GOD Is Talking; Are You Listening?

Accessing Your Akashic Record

For:

The Source is ready to communicate. Have you prepared yourself to listen?

With love,

GOD Is Talking; Are You Listening?

Accessing Your Akashic Record

Art Martin, Ph.D.

Personal Transformation Press
A Division of the Wellness Institute

GOD Is Talking; Are You Listening?
Accessing Your Akashic Record
Art Martin, Ph.D.

Published by
Personal Transformation Press
www.energymedicineinstitute.com
www.personaltransformationpress.com
mailforart@gmail.com

Copyright © 1999 Arthur H. Martin
Originally published as *Opening Communication with God Source*, June, 2000
Printed September, 2009

ISBN: 978-1-891962-18-9

Contents of this book are copyrighted. No part may be reproduced by mechanical means, photocopy or computer without written authorization of the publisher (except for brief quotations by reviewers).

This book explores the body/mind connection as the actual cause of all mental/emotional dysfunction and physical disease. However, the author in no way makes any diagnosis of medical condition or prescribes any medical treatment whatsoever.

Printed in the United States

Table Of Contents

Dedication vii
Acknowledgments ix
Preface xiii
Introduction xv

PART ONE: WHAT IS GOD?
    1. My Journey to Find GOD 1
    2. Are You Ready to Find GOD? 9
    3. Who Is the Presence of GOD? 13

PART TWO: GETTING PAST THE BLOCKS
    4. The Challenge of Clarity of Purpose 19
    5. The Mystery School of Life 23
    6. Connecting With Source 35
    7. The Use of Neuro-Kinesiology 39

PART THREE: ACCESSING THE AKASHIC
    8. What Is the Akashic Record? 49
    9. Accessing the Record I 53
    10. Accessing the Record II 57

PART FOUR: THE PATH
    11. The Meditation Process 61
    12. Building a Separate Reality 65
    13. Balanced Relaxation 67
    14. Forms of Meditation 69
    15. The Journal Technique 77
    16. Questions on The Process 99

PART FIVE: DIALOGUE WITH GOD SOURCE
    17. Communication with GOD Source 109
    Epilogue 163

APPENDICES
    A. The Practice of N/CR 175
    B. What Comprises An N/CR Session? 181
    C. Attitude Evaluation 185
    D. Books and Tapes 197
    E. Glossary 199
    About the Author 202

Other Books by Art Martin

Energy Psychology/Energy Medicine:
The Practice of Neuro-Kinesiology and
Psychoneuroimmunology
in Exploring the Mind/Body Connection

Becoming a Spiritual Being in a Physical Body

Your Body is Talking; Are You Listening?

2011 The New Millennium Begins

Recovering Your Lost Self

Journey Into the Light

Reparenting Yourself

Dedication

This book is dedicated to Paul Solomon.
He lit the light, showing the way to the Source.

Acknowledgments

Twenty years ago, when a prospective employee came into my restaurant to apply for a night manager job, little did I know that this man would be my first teacher. I could not understand why he was willing to sacrifice a well-paying job as a chemical engineer for a low-paying night job with no benefits. He was placid, easygoing and seemingly unflappable, and taught me many valuable lessons by example as well as conversationally.

In 1977, I decided to sell the restaurant and go on a journey to find myself, just as my friend had done, and I thank him so much for getting me on the path to transformation.

Later, while studying with Paul Solomon, I realized that the path was not going to be easy. Paul said, "Set your mind to it, and you will do it," and with the help of weekly *Course in Miracles* study groups at Jerry Jampolsky's office and seminars with Solomon and Beesley, I pulled through. On December 11, 1978, I made contact with The Source of My Being, thanks to Paul Solomon's guidance.

I will always be indebted to Paul for his insight and his determination to show us the way. My dialogue with the Source still continues today, with even greater clarity.

A Word on God

Since the topic of this book is communicating with the God Source, we must be clear what we mean by that term. For many years, the traditional concept of God was a sufficient definition for me, but I ran into trouble over this question: "If we are all talking to the same Source, why do we get so many different answers?"

After many long conversations with various sources, including the Source itself, I changed my viewpoint. In my conversations with Source, I noticed that it refers to itself as plural "we" rather than singular "I." Confused as to what this meant, I finally asked. This was the response:

"There is no 'I' nor do we represent a single Source of knowledge or information. We are a group consciousness. Unlike how the Christians look at their God, we are not a single being or entity. In fact your concept of God makes no sense in our terms, as we are not fundamentally different from you. The only difference between you and us is that we chose not to take bodies to experience the physical world. As you have discovered, doing so is fraught with perils, and most people do not have the discernment or discipline to experience your world without getting lost in the mire.

"You are a product of the same source as ourselves but, for your own purposes, you are not currently manifesting those qualities that identify a God-like being. The qualities lie dormant within you, but they have been overwritten with programs that block out your God-like qualities. However, you are currently in the process of reclaiming those qualities.

"So, again who is God and why do we refer to ourselves in plural? There is no one God being, and we refer to ourselves as 'we' because you may be communicating with more than one of our group at the same time. You may not be in contact with the same being each time you contact us. Depending on your question, one or other of our group may have more knowledge than others in that area, especially those who have returned from your world."

~ ~ ~

While this answer brought clarity, it presented me with a problem, for how could I use the term "God" without invoking the Christian concept of God as a single being? To avoid confusion, in this book, I use uppercase "GOD" to refer to the "Group Of Deities" that makes up the Source. Thus, it is not a single being in some high place called heaven. Further, since the group members have never taken physical bodies, they do not have gender, which is a quality peculiar to physical bodies.

Now, for some reason, people want to be able to use a name when in communication with them, but I have resisted that because I do not feel it is important, as long as I know *who* I am in communication with. So, whenever you see herein the term GOD, please remember that it refers a *group of high beings* that has chosen not to incarnate on the physical plane, but to serve from the higher dimensions. It is this group that Christians choose to worship as the singular entity they call "God."

Preface

My introduction to accessing the Akashic records was at an Inner Light Consciousness Seminar with Paul Solomon in 1978, in which he described a format involving meditation and visualization, a format I found to be extremely effective and workable.

Over the past twenty plus years of working with the records, I have witnessed many people who have demonstrated their abilities and personally experienced many forms of intuitive communication. Many people rely on their psychic abilities to access the records, but this is only reliable if the person is free of outside influences. Most people assume that all they need do is learn how to use their psychic abilities and they will be able to give readings. However, there is much more to giving *accurate* readings, such as exercising discretion as to *who* we allow to communicate with us, for when I started opening to my intuitive abilities, I was besieged by entities that wanted to open a channel with me.

My experience is that our extrasensory senses are more accurate if we follow a specific guiding protocol. As children, our extrasensory senses were developed, but our imprinters did not recognize them or disbelieved us when we described our experiences. As a result, most of us lost the ability to use those extrasensory abilities by the time we were five to seven years old. The purpose of this book is to describe how you can revive your dormant extrasensory abilities. I also present some of dialogues that I have had with the various GOD Sources.

When you access the Internet using your computer, you dial up your service provider, which then connects your computer to the web. Accessing the Akashic Internet is basically the same but you do not need to be wired into anything. Your higher self is your service provider and connects you to the records, to GOD Source, or to any other group or individual with whom you may want to communicate.

Sounds simple enough, but I have learned a few techniques that improve clarity and accuracy, and the intent of this book is to pass them onto you. The rest is then up to you.

Introduction

GOD Source is in everything, but we just don't recognize it. Its presence is in everyone, even though you may not be able to perceive it in yourself or other people because many of us have chosen to not manifest GOD-qualities or to suppress them by not living the qualities of honesty and integrity. Most people have lost sight of these qualities in their life.

Around 1980, frustrated by life's hardships, I was about to give up the spiritual path, feeling that if there was a God, then I should be taken care of. Each time I removed the programming in my body that was the cause of my physical problems, the pain kept returning. I was angry at having given my life to the service of teaching and healing others, but receiving the short shrift on everything. Astral forces were beating me up daily, and I was almost forced into bankruptcy when a group I trusted embezzled $30,000 from our bookstore/counseling center in an attempt to take it over and push me out. When that didn't work, they stole an $8,000 check that had been donated to the Wellness Institute to pay off some of the debts that they had incurred. We had to close the doors and go out of business. We lost our house and one of our cars. My remaining car seemed to break down or the engine would blow up for no apparent reason.

I had assumed that I was dealing with honest, trustworthy people but Spirit had other lessons for me. As a result, I became angry with God and any being from the White Brotherhood who was willing to listen. As the tribulations continued, I concluded that either God was ignoring my angry tirades or that there really was no God. Strangely, however, whenever I needed information about healing or therapy for my clients, I received immense help, but nothing for my own problems.

Having turned my back on the presence of God, I asked the highest source of my own being, my God-self, if it could connect me to extraterrestrial sources. "Who exactly do you want to talk with?" it asked, and I chose the Sirian Council. When I asked the Council for their view of God, the answer was a real eye-opener.

Their advice was, "Go back to your Source Consciousness and have another dialogue with God about what it is and how it functions in your life."

After a long dialogue with the Source Consciousness, I had to rethink my fundamental concepts. The Source Consciousness with whom I communicate turned out to be a group that calls itself the GOD Source. Furthermore, it is a Presence that resides in all of us.

I have listened to and read books by people who claim to be talking to God but, based on the information they are presenting, I have reservations about their sources. If you can read between the lines and carry on a dialogue with your Source at the same time, you can receive clear validation or otherwise about what you are reading. You can also discern insidious mind control information scattered throughout an otherwise excellent book without the author knowing what he or she was writing. The concepts may be well written, but certain key words that trigger mind control slip in unnoticed. I am not alone in this detecting this; many people have asked me whether they are reading more into a book than the author actually wrote, or are they reacting to some fear about the book's subject matter.

I often have the same experience while listening to a lecture. When I first had this experience, I thought my Judger sub-personality was trying to invalidate what I was hearing, so I worked at being able to differentiate between the Judger sub-personality and feedback from Source. Now that I have cleared all the Judger and Mind Controller sub-personalities, the content has become clear.

This happened recently when I was reading an article in *New Age* magazine about spirituality. Information flooded in so quickly that I had to write it down and soon realized that it was coming from Source. It clearly and concisely answered a longstanding question. The article made the point that most baby boomers are searching for a spiritual path, so they investigate many paths and religions but do not find satisfaction. The article's author remarked on the confusion these people experience because they are what she calls "spiritually promiscuous." That negative connotation did not sit well with me, for I feel that people should continue their search until they find something that works for them, so I put the question to the Source. Here is the answer:

"Most people confuse spirituality with the spiritual path. Many people want to be spiritual but do not know how to walk the path. They start following some spiritual practice or other, and think that is spirituality. It is not at all. Following some guru who created a dogma or practice, or some teacher who inherited the leadership of a spiritual path is not spirituality. It is a discipline that might lead to spirituality *if* it teaches followers to reclaim their personal power and self-validate, and the follower practices diligently. When you accept yourself and practice unconditional love and acceptance in your life, *and* you realize that you need no practice, ritual, teacher or guru, *then* you become the spiritual path." (Part 5: Dialogues with GOD Source goes into more detail on this topic.)

I think the challenge lies in the definition. People desire spirituality but think that by following a discipline or a ritual, they can somehow "get" spirituality. When we entered this life, we knew where we going, what we were going to do, and the lessons we had to learn. I stress this point in all my books many times; we must retrieve our flight plan so that we know what we must accomplish to get on the spiritual path. We must build a solid foundation for our spirituality, otherwise it will crumble or wilt at the first setback. Yet few people know what spirituality is, let alone can find the path to accomplish it.

We are all looking for a silver bullet that will enable us to feel better and accomplish our goals in life, yet we sink deeper in our misdirection, gathering concepts and ideas but never really finding spirituality. Many people who think they are already on the path are actually wandering about in a psychic wilderness. I have found this with many of my clients who feel they are on the path. If they are open enough to view their growth without delusion or denial, and we check to see how much progress they have made in their quest, we find they have been stalled at the door. As if they were caught in a revolving door, they think the path they have been on has yielded results, yet they have just been going in circles. They have yet to process the emotional trauma of childhood or the very reason why they entered life on this planet. The spiritual practice or path allowed them to skip building a solid foundation on which to base their spirituality. It's no wonder that these people feel unfulfilled because they're lulled into the delusion that the path they're on will yield a sense of completeness, yet the separation from self is still there. The illusion covered up true self and the unfinished lessons.

To begin any spiritual journey, we must lock the basics into our reality. They are peace, happiness, harmony, joy, unconditional love/acceptance and financial abundance. Few people have these basics locked down, yet they embark on a spiritual journey anyway.

Sometimes people become addicted to the search to the point where the search itself becomes their Holy Grail. The addiction can lead either to tunnel vision that shuts off any other opportunities, or to a never-ending search for the ultimate teacher, guru or master. Either way, such unhealthy attachment does not bring the much sought-after spirituality.

I spent many years looking for a path to God and a spiritual path that would yield the peace and happiness I desired, but I could not find it. All I found were empty disciplines and rituals. Many teachers said, "Follow me and I will show you the way," but all I found was control and quite often greed. "Follow me" really meant, "Pay me this much and I will show you the path." It's no different than the people in business and politics and their need for control and money. It's just given a spiritual label.

Eventually, however, I discovered one teacher who taught self-empowerment: Paul Solomon. He taught that all the information we need lies within our own Akashic Record, and it's available to us any time we decide to access it. This book is based on his teachings plus my research over two decades. The spiritual journey described merges the spiritual path and your knowingness that results in a spirituality that encompasses your whole being. I found the path and the GOD that supports my journey. It is all within you. It is not a ritual but a practice in which you live your life as the Presence of GOD would. *That* is spirituality. Once you can access the knowledge that is available to all of us, it is very simple.

Contrary to popular belief, the Akashic Records are not all stored outside the body. They are composed of any action you take that creates a record, past, present or future. They are a 24/7 bookkeeping system that records every thought, feeling, emotion, action, reaction or response, and through what is called the Collective Mind, we can access all its records.

We were born fully equipped to access the Akashic Record, and all we need do is turn on the switch. Our Subconscious Mind's computer came ready to access the Collective Mind, and we were born with all the instructions on how to do so, only we forgot that we even have this information. All we need is the discipline to learn, as when we buy a new software program. Once we learn the new software and how to activate it, using it is very easy.

The best way to access the Akashic is through active meditation. To connect with your Higher Self, you must commit to a regular session each day, for familiarity establishes a pattern, much like learning to type.

Past lives are stored in our Akashic Record in the Subconscious Mind's computer files. Every time we enter a life, we simply continue the same journey. In fact, you begin where you ended your journey in the previous life. You cannot "jump over" the lessons you lay out for yourself. Your lesson plan drives your life, as do all the core beliefs created from the past.

We are entitled to peace, happiness, harmony and joy with unconditional love, abundance and prosperity in our lives, and the whole road map for achieving them is laid out. But we decide how we are going to handle a particular lesson, and may spend many lifetimes going down a dead-end road without even knowing it. However, to resume course, all we need do is access the information in the Akashic Record.

The Akashic Record contains all the instructions and the methods to obtain exactly the life you want, but the catch is that you must read it. Nobody else—therapists, readers, psychics—can cause anything to happen for you, even if they can read the records for you. They can guide you to the right path, but *you must do the work*. That is why it's so important to be able to access the Akashic records yourself.

I talk about the Subconscious Mind's "computer" but there is not a computer company that could build a computer remotely like the Subconscious Mind. Not only is its storage capacity unlimited, but it can also process many tracks of complex information simultaneously, such as thinking, listening to music, holding a conversation, and driving a car all at the same time, and each of the trillions of cells of our bodies is a networking computer that works with the four main computers that comprise our minds, yet we need pay nothing for this miraculous service, or wait to get online. A simple affirmation is all that's needed.

Any answer is available to any question. If money seems to elude you, ask about the base cause. Once you find that, you can access the core issues, core beliefs, and encoded or encrypted records or messages. You may also need to rewrite a basic program in the Subconscious Mind's computer. One of these programs may have locked you into following a certain path and must be deleted and destroyed before you can get back on track.

There are many ways to access the records, some more reliable than others. The challenge is to be sure we are clear, and to recognize that we are "on-line" with the right source, for many masqueraders would like to convince you that they are your spirit guides, yet they are nothing more than mischievous discarnate spirits.

Many psychics claim that they're able to tap into the right source, but often astral plane entities intervene because the psychics are not going via their Higher Selves. This book will show you the specific actions you must take to be sure you are clear and can get online without interference, or without some outside entity cutting in on your line and masquerading as your

Higher Self, spirit guide, or even the presence of GOD. We must know how to go through the astral plane to the higher dimensions, or we will suffer interference from earthbound and astral-bound entities, dark forces, and other entities that want to be your spirit guides. Until we get clear of all intervening influences, we cannot be sure with whom we are communicating.

If all psychics have a clear line, why is it that the same question elicits different answers from each? More than likely, they do *not* have a clear line to the Source. Their own minds may be filtering the information, or they may be experiencing interference. However, the good news is that we each have an immense reservoir of knowledge of which we're unaware. There is only one clear way into the Akashic—the Presence of GOD that communicates directly through your Higher Self—and the quality of the communication verifies whether or not you're online to the genuine thing. This book will reveal the specific questions to ask to get the source to identify itself.

For example, I often ask an entity to identify "the August Body." If it can answer that question with the proper identity, I'm sure that I have an authentic connection to the Source. If the entity hedges, I know that it is not online with the Highest Source. (All enlightened beings in the higher dimensions know that the August Body is a mystery school based on ancient Pythagorean principles. You will never find this school or be admitted to it without an invitation. The people who run this school will evaluate your work and contact you if they want to interview you.)

Your body will also reveal whether the psychic is clear. Muscle testing is an excellent way to reveal whether he or she is free of the need to be right and any personal agenda. This book describes how to do this.

So, I welcome you to a fascinating journey of discovery that will put you in touch with the wisdom of your soul and much more. You can read the book quickly to get the lay of the land and then go back for a more thorough pass, or you can slowly savor each chapter as the journey unfolds. Either way, I honor you for taking this incredible journey with me.

PART ONE

WHAT IS GOD?

1

My Journey to Find GOD

When I was a teenager, I wondered why my parents did not attend church. My mother explained why. Her grandfather had been a Methodist minister and her mother had converted to a Four Square Gospel church and was always out saving drunks and battling for prohibition. They even lived in a red light district in Los Angeles so her mother could do her ministry with the women of the night. As a result, my mother, being the oldest child of eight, ended up being the mother to the family, since her mother didn't appreciate that her children were more important than saving the rest of humanity.

My mother came to resent the demands placed on her and blamed organized religion, which she'd had pushed on her for many years. As a result, I was never baptized, and many religions told me I was not "saved." At the time, I refused to buy into the born-again Christian concept even though I did try some of the conservative churches and bought into the Christian God concept.

After a few Roman Catholic services, I took an immediate dislike to the Church. It seemed to me the congregation was being controlled by fear and guilt. The sermons in Latin didn't make

Catholicism approachable, either. I tried a few fundamentalist churches but was turned off by their zealous dogma, and most mainstream churches didn't offer what I sought. Eventually, I settled on a Presbyterian church, but when I saw all the unethical behavior by both the minister and some of the church members, I even dropped out of that, my interest in religion a thing of the past.

In college, I took some courses in theology and comparative religion, which opened my eyes to the other world religions. When some of the students in the class tried to argue the Christian viewpoint over the other religions, I was relieved that the instructor refused to let them. But their behavior finally turned me against the dogmatic, fundamentalist Christian viewpoint.

In 1963, many religious groups were starting clubs on campus. As the student body president, I let them do so if they did not preach any dogma and were open to all, without discrimination. The Catholic group invited me to their off-campus meeting, where they discussed the pros and cons of birth control, a hot topic since many drug companies were researching birth control pills and the Roe v. Wade abortion decision was before the Supreme Court.

I was surprised that the Catholic group would even discuss the matter in view of their Church's position, although I knew how the debate would conclude. However, during the heated discussion, my friend posed the question, "Many countries in the world have few activities open to their citizens, so sex is the major recreation for many. The result is often large families that they cannot support. Do you really believe that God would approve of your position when it is creating so much hunger and strife in these countries?" The priest gave such a poor defense for the church's position that many in the audience were shocked.

The next month's topic, suggested by a friend, was to be another controversial subject: "Is the church man-created or divinely created by God?" Because I was on the college debate team, I was appointed to the three-man team speaking on behalf of the man-created argument. However, the other two dropped out because they did not want to offend the Church's viewpoint, so I ended up arguing the man-created side alone.

Two of the opposing debaters also dropped out, leaving another non-club member to argue the divine-created side, a position he did not support, so ironically two non-Catholics ended up debating a Catholic matter before a group of Catholics. I won the debate because my opponent could offer no evidence that God had anything to do with the creation of the Church. I, on the other hand, was able to present documented evidence that charismatic leaders such as the apostle Paul were behind all religions.

Word had got around the college about the debate so we had a large turnout, and for weeks afterwards, people plied me with questions about the subject. To many people, I was Mr. Anti-religion, which was not true at all. I was still searching for the truth, but was sure that I would not find it in a Christian church.

For the next 14 years, I eschewed organized religion, but still had plenty of heated discussions along the way. Eventually, I did find another church that was interesting, with a minister who was open and willing to listen. The services were unique in that there was no sermon. Instead, lay people read passages from the Bible and the minister acted as a moderator for a congregation discussion. My wife, Susie, became a Sunday school teacher and we became really involved. I spent many hours exchanging viewpoints with the minister, who understood my skepticism but said if he were to openly support me, he would be asked to leave.

One memorable Sunday, many people couldn't understand the biblical passage, and the minister was unable to shed any light either. At that moment, a strong voice said to me, "Can we talk through you? We have the explanation."

"Who are you?" I asked.

"You will recognize who we are when we explain the passage," the voice explained.

I agreed, and when the voice finished its explanation, the source was obvious: the being we know as Jesus Christ. He made many direct statements such as, "It may be written that way but that is not what I intended to say."

Needless to say, the conversation was a mind-bender. Over the following months, the minister received many complaints about the viewpoint I expressed, which proves to me that if Jesus walked into a church today, they would probably not accept him. So that was the end of that church.

After a while, I thought that I'd finally found a church that fitted my viewpoint, and entered a lay minister-training program to become an assistant minister. Susie again became a Sunday school teacher. The church had been a Unity Church, but the Unity movement did not approve of the new minister because he was not Unity-trained, so we changed the name to Creative Living Center. The congregation grew from less than a hundred people meeting in an old gym to over three thousand with a beautiful facility that had regular offices and classrooms. In six years, he took the Center from a struggling, disorganized few to a large, dynamic successful organization.

Unfortunately, after three years, a new board was elected that began to erode the whole program. They began deducting rent from the minister's salary and charging people who wanted to see him, claiming that because he was doing psychological therapy, he should pay for office space and charge for appointments. He wanted to be a full time minister, but the board cut his salary so he had to find an outside job to supplement his income, so many of his pastoral programs died.

Within short three years, the board of directors forced the minister to resign, and he joined one of the largest Science Of Mind Churches in the U.S. in Arcadia, CA. The Center now has fewer than 75 members and rents a shopping mall storefront.

In 1982, Susie and I attended a teacher-training program with Paul Solomon in Virginia Beach, VA that led to a ministerial certificate and a Doctor of Divinity degree, which allowed me to serve as a substitute minister in many churches.

We joined another Unity Church in the Sacramento, CA area, and Susie became a Sunday school teacher and an advisor to a youth program. However, the same political infighting soon broke out, and the board asked the current minister to leave. As a result, a large faction of the church left to form another group. We stuck it out for a while but in 1990, the board would not renew the minister's contract, so she formed a new church about 15 miles away and took many with her.

Throughout the succession of new ministers, I kept coming into conflict with the church over my beliefs, and was barred from conducting sermons, even though many of my clients attended the church and raved about my work and my new concepts. But when I, a professional healer, was excluded from a weekend healing seminar, that was the end of me and organized religion.

So what's this all about? My experience with organized religion over the last fifty years has been abysmal. Dedicated to looking for a form of God, I was not finding it in churches. What I did find was many people who wanted to control the activities of others and did not practice the spiritual principles they preached, such as love and forgiveness. Very few followed the simple rules that Christ laid down 2,000 years ago. Sadly, even the churches seem to have lost sight of basic spiritual laws, and are degenerating into control, authority and greed for power over others.

Turning to the Bible, I am also dismayed at the portrayals of the vengeful God of the Old Testament Hebrews, and wonder who this God was and whether he really had treated these people in this manner—another reason to avoid organized religion.

Few people know that the Bible that we use today is actually a Roman Catholic Bible, or that prior to a conference in Nicea in 321 AD, there was no Bible. At the conference, the Pope, cardinals and Emperor Constantine, along with the bishops and their advisors, surveyed all available contemporary writings, and selected 66 to go into the collection they termed "The Holy Bible." An equal number of writings were omitted that had any reference to anything that would empower the people.

Further research uncovered something called "The Jesus Project," a group of prominent theological college professors who got together to investigate the historical accuracy of Jesus' life. Their findings were amazing.

They discovered that a person by name of Jesus Christ never existed, and that his life was fabricated by the Conference of Nicea as a rehash of much older myths, such as those of Krishna and Horus. Apparently, they created the mythical being called Jesus so they could have a figurehead to bolster their church's position against its competitors. Most major religions have a figurehead, such as a prophet, to serve as spokesperson for the organization, so why not create one for the Christians?

Weaving in a little documented history for credibility, the bishops concocted the story of virgin birth to a woman called Mary. This was easy to do since in Greek, Mary was a "virgo," meaning that she had not yet born a child. After a simple translation "error," however, subsequent generations proclaimed that Mary was a virgin, and since only the priest class could read, no one else knew any different.

Also woven into the myth were men such as Appolonius of Tyana, who was described as a Teacher of Righteousness. He was a true ascended being as he could dematerialize at will, which frustrated the Romans because he could easily evade them and just pop up somewhere else. In view of the almost identical life stories, Appolonius seems to have been the basis of the mythical Paul character.

This material may shock someone who accepts the Jesus myth without question. In fact, when I first heard it, I checked it out with the Source, and surprisingly received confirmation.

In studying how the current Bible has been "massaged" and mistranslated over the last 1,700 years, I found all types of errors and manipulations made by various leaders, most recently in the King James Version, allegedly reworked by freemason Francis Bacon (also suspected by scholars also to be the real author of Shakespeare's works). The history of the Bible reveals many distorted interpretations and shifted meanings of some of the most important issues. The most accurate version is the Jerusalem Bible.

Where did my search lead me?

As you can see, I did not find the God of the Christians, but as you read this book, you will understand what I *did* find—a group of individuals who represent the *presence* of GOD. I also questioned them in my quest to understand who we are and how we can relate with the GOD Source.

Eventually I found what I sought, and derive comfort from knowing that we can achieve GOD's level of awareness if we discipline ourselves to follow the spiritual journey to its end. This allows us to trade the world of competition, control, manipulation, and strife for a world of peace, joy, harmony, happiness, and peace. We can do it right here on this planet, now.

In the last two years, my travels and the events that have transpired around me have proved that it is possible. I am following the directions and the path given in my book *Journey Into the Light*, and so far it seems to be working well. You may not agree with what I have found, but that's all right. Follow what works for you.

In any situation, ask yourself what redeeming factor is this providing for me? Does it provide unconditional love and abundance? Am I getting peace, happiness, joy, and harmony from this path? Am I satisfied with my progress on my spiritual journey? Are other people validating me and what I do?

In the end, you are looking for complete satisfaction with your life. Do you live with grace and ease, or do you have to drive and push your way through life? If the latter, then maybe you need to rethink your direction and get on a spiritual journey that *does* provide the rewards you want from life. The main obstacles are our own illusions and denials. If we can evaluate our path correctly and with self-honesty, we can stay on the path. Many people claim to be advanced in their spiritual journey, yet a Kinesiology test reveals little progress on their path.

The only part of your mind that avoids and denies the truth is your conscious mind, which is either under your control or on autopilot. All the other parts of your mind will tell the truth if you will allow them to do so. We will return to this issue later in the book.

2

Are You Ready To Find GOD?

In my quest to find God (I didn't know about GOD at the time), I met many people who were intensely afraid of God because their church had told them that they were sinners whom God would judged harshly unless they accepted Jesus Christ as the only way to salvation. On the opposite side, I met Humanists, who believe this is the one-and-only life and we are our own salvation.

I fell somewhere between the two extremes because I was looking for a forgiving God and was convinced there was some universal plan devised by some CEO. Whilst not an atheist, I did reject the existence of the God touted by the major religions.

In my passionate search for truth, I read four books a week and diligently practiced *A Course In Miracles*. In my twice-daily meditations, I asked to make contact with the Holy Spirit or the Presence of God, but nothing happened for almost nine months other than spirits that intruded, claiming to be spirit guides and angels among other things. But I knew that they were not the highest source, so I refused to deal with them. Then, on December 11, 1978, the veil was lifted, when I heard a voice say, "We are here now."

"Who are you?" I asked, but no identification was offered. Then, two weeks later, the voice finally identified itself as the Source. Once I learned how to effectively dialogue with them, they would spend two to four hours a day answering my questions, and the nature of GOD as a group emerged.

I was surprised to find that their answers made no reference to what religious writers and theologians called God. For example, one Sunday, I watched a church minister exhort the angels of God to bless us, and was amazed to see several angels actually manifest right next to the podium where he was speaking. I asked them, "Are you real or figments of my imagination?"

Their answer blew me away because, at the time, I had only been in the field of spirit communication for about a year. They replied, "Why did he call us here and then ignore us? Does he really understand what he's doing or is he just doing this because he was told that it's what he is supposed to do? We are here, so what does he want us to do now?"

My response was, "I don't think he really knows what he is doing. He seems to go by the book. This obviously was not spontaneous."

So, although I was talking to the Source, I was not sure what that really was. Even though Paul Solomon had assured us that we were talking to God, I had my reservations about the whole process. I had seen so many people who claimed to talk with ascended masters, spirit guides, and other named beings, yet their communications did not seem to have any real value that I could see.

Not wanting to fall into the same trap, when people asked me to read for them, I refused. Also, I wasn't sure of my ability, so I reserved it for myself. However, I would take their questions and ask them in private. When I later relayed the answers, people verified their accuracy so my confidence slowly began to build up and I began doing live readings. Within a year, I was on the phone from 5 to 8 a.m. most days of the week. By 1980, I had become what today we call a medical intuitive, and was providing information on how to heal almost every form of illness and disease, both in person and over the phone.

When I was in college working on my psychology degree, I became disappointed because, although I gave people the information they needed, they rarely benefited from it. I wondered why this was. The response was that programming locked into the body's cellular memory controls all illness and disease.

So my question to GOD was, "If you are so all-powerful, as people say you are, why can't you heal them?"

That triggered many lively discussions that led me to develop Neuro/Cellular Reprogramming. Along the way, I discovered that behind *all* dysfunction—no matter if just held in the mind or at the stage of physical disease—was an original cause that could be identified and dealt with. At this point, I stopped doing psychic readings and shifted my focus to finding the malfunctioning programs in the mind's computers.

Despite being an effective psychological counselor, I decided that it was a waste of my time and was not getting lasting results for my clients. Sometimes it did work if the client had a intense commitment to follow the instructions, but usually, we could find the cause but we were unable to heal the disease, illness or dysfunction. Why were only some people getting healed yet they all had the answer? This led me deeper into what happens during healing and how the power of GOD could be used to heal people.

My research consistently showed that, although we *are* GOD, most people cannot conceive that they could be GOD-like. Christians have placed their God on such a high pedestal that it's completely out of reach. In fact, many of them strongly resented me even making the comparison, and I got into many heated discussions over this question. Some went so far as claiming I was demonically possessed, or the Antichrist, even. So, although I had developed a healing process with documented results, my recipe for health was not popular with many people, and my faith was shaken by all the dissension about my success.

So, I ask you to look in the mirror, and if you can't see GOD, then I suggest that you clean up your act. You are GOD and you are a co-creator of this universe as it is now. So it's time you began to tap into your GOD-like qualities and started on your spiritual journey now. Forgiveness is the key. Forgiveness for ourselves and our soiled past.

Are you ready to find you?

3

Who Is the Presence of GOD?

For several years, I was skeptical about whether there even was a God, but now I know GOD is not a single individual but a group that includes each of us. We are all GOD but very few people actually exhibit GOD-like qualities. We are all on a search to return to where we were when we fell from grace, although few spiritual paths teach this. So how does this affect my view of GOD?

In the seventies, *A Course in Miracles* and Jerry Jampolsky's weekly study groups gave me a different slant on a God that forgave us no matter what we did in the past. It was a hard concept to understand but those weekly study groups helped and, in 1984, I started a study group myself that still meets today.

Also in 1984, I met Neale Donald Walsh, the author of *Conversations With God*, and sponsored a few workshops for him in the mid-eighties. He had just written a small book titled *Hitler Went To Heaven*, and the first sentence of the introduction hit me: "This is not about Hitler going to heaven at all. It is about your willingness to forgive Hitler for what he did."

That changed my views about God. I now had someone who validated my emerging understanding of God, which led me closer to my concept of GOD. Many people talk about forgiveness without understanding what it really means. Forgiveness is *acceptance without any judgment whatsoever*. Many people operate from *selective forgiveness*, and often want something in return for their forgiveness—a trade, if you will. True forgiveness is unconditional—no withholds or conditions.

I feel that the lack of genuine forgiveness is at the root of what is wrong with the world today. People are looking out for their own survival to the point that they will lie, cheat, and act out of integrity, yet find nothing wrong with their behavior. We need look no further than our elected public officials, from the local to national levels. Where does GOD fit into all this? If people would simply follow the teachings attributed to the mythical Jesus figure, we would have a safer and more honest world. Some of the biggest offenders are the pious Christian politicians, and I ask you, what kind of example are they setting for the young people of this world? I am irritated when I see our alleged leaders acting without honor and integrity, and then denying any accusations of wrongdoing, convinced that what they are doing is right. All I can do is forgive them, knowing that they are not aware of what they are doing.

Once in a lecture, at the height of the Lewinski scandal, someone asked me, "What do you feel about what's going on in Washington?" The Source stepped in and answered, "What is happening with Clinton and Congress is a barometer of what is happening in the U.S. The politicians are an out-picturing of the consciousness of the country. People do not want the Clinton affair to be dragged out because it brings up their own guilt and misdeeds. The more the scandal becomes public, the more it affects the citizens' views of themselves. Most people are in denial of their behavior, just as Clinton is. They want this affair over so they can bury their denial and continue on automatic pilot."

Returning to the question of the Presence of GOD, I sometimes have difficulty in following the tenets set down in the various dialogues I have with GOD Source Consciousness. They have basically defined a life path for me, yet sometimes I backslide a little. (My book *Journey Into the Light* documents much of my struggle.) But once I was able to clear the Judger sub-personalities out of my programming, I found following the path much easier. The clearer I got, the more smoothly my life operated.

Two of my books discuss the subject of clearing, but I will recap it here because of its importance in this discussion. In the beginning, we were all sparks of light. We lived in a state of grace, with no need to control, compete or manipulate. However, we could not resist the temptation to experience physicality and its sensuous pleasures. We were warned what might happen if we got lost in physicality, but didn't listen and got lost. We are now far removed from our original spark of light state, but many deny that we are and, as a result, they fall even farther from the path. In fact, most people don't even know that a path actually exists. With some people, attitudes prevail along the lines of, "He who dies with the most toys wins," "Hit it in this life as that's all there is," "Take advantage as often as you can," "Do whatever you must to get to the top," "Do unto others before they do it unto you," "Take all you can get if no one is watching," and "Say whatever you want to justify your actions." Many people are pathological liars, yet people allow them to get away with it all the time. The Law of Karma, or cause-and-effect simply doesn't exist in these people's minds.

Those of us who are trying to follow the spiritual journey see many of our fellow travelers lost in denial. It is our responsibility to help those who have made a commitment to get on the path, even though they may not have the full picture yet. But if we were once sparks of light, can we get back there? Yes, we can but it's going to take hard work because we have dropped to a very low ebb. However, we cannot help those who are in denial and refuse to see that they need help.

Other planetary groups I have communicated with consider Earth to be the garbage dump of the universe, and that everyone who has dropped to the bottom of the barrel is on this planet. If that is so, we have a big job on our hands.

American politicians exemplify why we are the universal garbage dump. For example, a caller to a radio talk show asked, "If a person is lying and you know that he is, but you also know the actual facts in the matter, then is this actually a lie?"

The talk show host asked the caller for clarification. Apparently, the caller wanted to vindicate Clinton by claiming since everyone knew he was lying and was not fooling anybody, then he really wasn't lying, as though it was all some kind of game. This is the kind of false, twisted reasoning under which many people in this country operate. Few people understand the law of cause-and-effect, or karma: "What goes around comes around."

The attorneys defending Clinton admitted he broke the law, adding, "but it's not that bad." With a survival mentality, you do whatever you must to survive. If you can get away with it, then do it. In the words of Jesus, "Forgive them for they do not know what they are doing."

In my recent dialogues with the Source, I have been getting feedback that we must change the way people are operating. The old concept of, "Do unto others before they can do unto you," must go. Trying to shift the blame off yourself so that you can avoid dealing with the truth has to end. A major house cleaning appears inevitable in the next few years, something I hope people are ready for.

In my search for a God that I could look up to, what I found was us. But how many of us are living the tenets and teachings of the true Presence of GOD? Not enough, I'm afraid. Many are in the process of waking up, which is good news, and when the numbers reach critical mass, we will see a major shift in consciousness on this planet. But we need to awaken many more people before we make a major change in how people function.

A radio talk show host once asked his audience, "Why don't you sheeple wake up to what's happening?" But most people missed the point of his penetrating question because they are asleep at the wheel and operating on autopilot.

I often ask the various beings with whom I communicate, "What has happened to the values of ethics, integrity and honesty?" They are appalled that we have been drawn into the mire and are lost in the greed, control and the unethical behavior prevalent on our planet, as happened when we originally fell from grace many millennia ago. Wherever you are on your evolutionary journey, you can still backslide if you can't resist the temptations of greed, control, power, and manipulation.

We are the Presence of GOD, and the extraterrestrials I communicate with tell me that we must return to an ethical life based on integrity and honesty. When we grasp that, we will see a major shift in consciousness in business, government, and the general population. It may take a while for this to happen, but it is inevitable as we move toward the dimensional shift. However, we must stop looking outside of ourselves for our spirituality. As the old saying goes, "If you need something to believe in, start believing in yourself."

When I ask the extraterrestrials for their opinion, they point me back to our history and show me how, whenever the planet falls out of balance, a major catastrophe wipes the slate clean and we start over again. Earth is not the only planet where this happens. It is a universal lesson that all cultures go through in their evolution. As a relatively young planet in relation to others in the galaxy, Earth is destined to go through these growing pains as we once more approach this cleansing.

Many scientists, historians, and anthropologists have documented geological shifts that apparently happened in less than a day, and I asked my sources, "If there is a loving GOD, then why would they allow this to happen?" The usual answer is, "Each planet has its own lessons and consequences to work through in its evolution. Since your planet is in a sense the garbage dump of the universe, it is the work planet where all karma is worked out. Souls come here to work out their karma and rectify the past. You create your own reality. That is why you are on this planet. Do not expect someone to clean it up for you. It is your responsibility. You are the presence of GOD, and you know the proper path to take. You just have to find it. That is the key. When you drop the 'poor me,' and all the fear, anger, and resentment, you will find the path. Of course, you can choose to stay in indecision, procrastinate, and refuse to take responsibility. But you are here for a reason, and if you cannot see anything out of place in your life, you should start looking at your denial. You need to wake up to that fact, or you may be passing to the next work planet after this planet moves up to the fifth dimension. We take care of our own and cannot take care of those who get lost in your mire."

We are a multidimensional, multicultural society that is a collection of souls from all over the galaxy trying to work out karma. We were sent here by the Lords of Karma to work out our differences. According to the planetary beings from many galaxies and star systems with whom I have communicated, we are not doing a very good job of waking up since less than 10 percent of our population is getting the message. That is a sad commentary when you view the downward spiral that happening. There still is hope, however, as more people get the message each day.

Our skies are full of extraterrestrials, yet our governments strive to cover up all the sightings and communication. In fact, many people who are in the know who have either left or continue in government position are afraid to say anything for fear they might be destroyed. It is a sad commentary that so many people live in fear of so many sources, including their God.

Whenever I talk with the GOD Source, I get the same answers. So where does that leave me in my quest for the true GOD? Join me in my search in the rest of these pages.

PART TWO

GETTING PAST THE BLOCKS

4

The Challenge of Clarity of Purpose

One of the hardest aspects in finding the right path is making sure that you are clear of influences from all outside sources, such as misdirected or unclear spirit guides, dark forces, extraterrestrial or alien attachments, conscious mind chatter, and sub-personality influences that will control or affect your answers. Illusion surrounds us and we can buy into it very easy, especially as most of the world is living in illusion. What we think we see as the truth may very well be an illusion.

When I was studying alternative therapies and the various spiritual paths in the late seventies and early eighties, most of them failed to deliver what I was looking for when I put them to the test. Since I was not clear of control, attachments, fear, anger and all the other garbage that can give you false reads, getting accurate and appropriate information was a real battle. However, when the dawn started breaking and I was able to see clearly, it was not hard to find the right path.

You may get the answer you desire, but it may not be the true answer, and if your ability to be clear is clouded, you will not recognize that it is happening. If your illusion is about your need to be right or seeking personal validation, no one will be able to convince you that you're not getting clear answers. The main addictions we humans all have are to be right and be in control, and we will do anything to remain in control and defend our actions. It's easy for outside observers to see what's going on for you if they are clear, but even though it's obvious to others, we will not see it as long as we fear not being in control. So the main challenge is to validate the information you are channeling or the answers you are bringing forth.

We are all clairvoyant; all we need do is sharpen our abilities and let go of the fear. We teach this in a workshop, and it is easy to pick up and work with once you let go of your fear or the need to be an authority and in control.

I have attended many lectures given by people who claim to be a clear channel for some entity, yet when I monitor their source, I get unclear signals. Many times the information is correct until a subtle intrusion intervenes. When I spot the influence of misdirection, I get concerned that the accurate information is being given merely as a subterfuge to cover up some dark force or alien agenda. Or we can lock into what we think is a true spirit guide when we are actually in contact with a person who passed over and is looking for someone to communicate through. This can happen when we do not direct our intention to the Highest Source of our being.

A good example of this happened at a workshop that was presented for me by a Los Angeles bookstore around 1990. The owner had been giving psychic readings for many years so I invited him to our workshop the following weekend. During the workshop, we cleared the owner of all outside forces, possessive beings, etc., and the next week, he told me that he could no longer do readings and asked what we did to foul up his channel. I told him that all we did was to clear a possessive spirit being that was attached to him—obviously the source of his channeling. There is no reason to let any being take over or be in control of your mind or body. We must to be careful not to invite dark forces from the astral plane to us in an effort just to get a channel or spirit guide.

We must protect ourselves when we open up in meditation or in any form of psychic or clairvoyant work, for I have found that even encircling myself with white light does not work effectively. People claim that many rituals work but I have found that they are no defense against powerful astral forces that have no recognition of honesty, integrity or ethics. Anything goes in their world. Many people will invoke the power of God or Jesus Christ, but you must also be at a level of consciousness where that works. It does not work for everyone.

The only sure protection I have found is the Body/Mind Harmonizer that we developed specifically for this purpose. It operates at the same frequency as the Arc of the Covenant, and wards off any outside forces and stops intervention of any form, including psychic attack and cording by other people. (See Appendix C for information on this device.)

Kinesiology is subject to the same controlling effects. If you are not clear or have clouded attachments on you, your ability to discern the truth will be compromised. (In Chapter 7 on Muscle Testing, we discuss the safeguards necessary in using Kinesiology.)

Any divination process can *appear* to give you right answers because they are coming directly and immediately, but are they correct? Your mind or outside forces can always compromise dowsing, pendulums, and muscle testing, as we frequently find among attendees at our workshops and lectures. (The pendulum is the easiest form to control, and we must be sure that our mind or outside forces are not influencing our answers.)

When we master this, we must look at our life and the journey we are on. Many delude themselves that they are on the spiritual path, yet they still function without ethics and integrity. Many want to be on the path and the spiritual journey, yet they continue to procrastinate, hesitate, muddle in indecision and refuse to take their power back and commit to responsibility. These people obviously know the rules of the road and how to get there, and all they need do is listen to their conversations about the spiritual path and what they should be doing to realize that they are not walking their talk. Again, this comes back to discernment and committed action. How many "no limit" people do you know who are driving forward in their lives and making their mark in this world?

5

The Mystery School of life

We often get to a place in life where we know that we must make a decision to change. Life is not providing the rewards or the peace, happiness, harmony and joy that we seek. Sometimes, we have been on the spiritual path for thirty years or more, yet life is not providing the feeling of accomplishment we feel it should. When you recognize this, what do you do? Run to psychics and see if they can provide you with the path. Few will be able to, for it is an inner job.

The main detour is illusion and control sub-personalities that are tied into denial and denial-of-denial. Your mind can play some real games with you if you have given all your control to autopilot. The longer you have operated from Middle Self and the sub-personalities, the more entrenched they are. Autopilot programs do not give up control very easily. They will fight for their control almost as if they are not part of you, and can cause a loss of identity to the point where multiple or split personalities can take over.

Clarity is of the utmost importance, as we saw in the previous chapter. In the ancient mystery schools, the first lesson in the curriculum was learning to be silent and listen. In fact, you had to take a vow of silence to enter the school. You were not allowed to ask questions or talk with anyone at all during the time you were attending the school. You were not allowed to bring anything to the school, either. You had to let go of all attachments, including communication with anyone outside of the school.

How many people could meet those conditions today? Very few. Letting go of attachments can be frightening, as change can be to those who have been on autopilot most of their lives. You must get to a point where you are willing to discipline yourself and make the decision to step into a new reality, to step out of the rut you are in, and discipline yourself to step forward and reach out to a new way of life. If you know the steps, it's not a mystery because it's all laid out before you. The question is: can you listen to the dialogue and release the fear so that you can take the steps?

Teachers appear in your life but you may not want to listen or take their advice. You may have considerable fear/anger and resistance to taking the advice. If the teacher appears when the student is ready, the challenge is to recognize the teacher. You may have preconceptions as to what the teacher should look like, but true teachers seldom appear as we think they should.

My 25-year search for my teachers brought some interesting experiences. First, I had to learn to be open to evaluating their information. We must also know when it's time to move on, and I attribute my success partly to my not stopping when I found a process that worked, because I knew that I did not yet have all the pieces to the puzzle. Even today, I continue to attend other people's lectures and seminars looking for more tools. However, many people master one process and feel that because they have found a process that works, their search is over.

I have found it important to be open to all avenues that come our way. There may be detours among the paths that are right for you, and you must use discernment. The lesson may be right in front of you, but any illusion or denial will block you from the truth. But if you have the eyes to see and the ears to hear, you will see the lesson clearly.

There may be times when you do not want to take on the responsibility or pursue the direction indicated, even thought you know deep down that this is the path you must take as the next step in your spiritual journey. It is all about desire, discipline and constant, consistent determined action. Most people live in the illusion that everything in their life is all right. Many who consider themselves on the path think that their lives are working, yet they still lack peace, happiness, harmony, joy, unconditional acceptance, and abundance in their lives. If you are willing to settle for a mediocre level of health and wellness, accepting limitations is a choice you make. But when you decide you want to be a "no-limit person" and become results-oriented, your life will change.

In Paul Solomon's workshops and seminars, many people talked a good line about what they were going to do with the teachings, but 20 years later, most of them have fallen by the wayside, leading basically the same life they did 20 years ago. A few have new awareness and are shining examples of the application of the principles, yet most did nothing even though Paul gave us all the principles of the mystery schools and told us how to achieve the goals of evolution and transformation. What does that tell you?

Many people I have worked with have used the suggestions from my workshops and in my books and changed the direction of their lives. The material in this book may make me look as if I am setting myself up as the ultimate authority, but I don't consider myself a guru, shaman or any other special person. All I do is show clients what they must do to achieve results in their life. Of course, this information is all laid out in the clients' flight plans that they filed before birth.

If you have gone through some detours, I can show you how to get back on your spiritual journey. You can do this if you are clear enough the read the records, as we have already discussed. However, the lessons and discipline can be hard to handle at times. We can become a "no limit person" but it takes desire, determination, consistent discipline, and the committed willingness to stay with the lessons even when the going gets tough. Most people give up and go on a detour and/or escape into denial. To get the real you to emerge takes commitment and work. Many times we must take on a task or follow through with something that we do not want to do because we know this is the next step in our path to transformation.

The following case studies demonstrate how lessons are presented to us. Each one is about self-empowerment and reclaiming personal power. The final result is the same but you will see each person took a different path to get to the goal.

Joseph was born in China during the Depression. His father was in the import sales business, and when World War II broke out, Joseph and his mother returned to the States. His father lost his business and returned to the States when hostilities forced him out, but he never recovered from this blow and became sick, basically withering away in the hospital.

Joseph's mother went blind when he was four years old, so he became her "guide dog" and had little of a normal childhood. Furthermore, his mother was negative, and freely told her son that she never wanted to have a child in the first place. As with many children who have been rejected in this way, he ended up sick much of the time in an attempt to elicit the attention he needed from his mother. She resented his neediness, and rejected him even more.

To alleviate his asthma, Joseph and his mother moved to Florida for its climate but it made no change because he still wasn't getting the love, acceptance and validation from his mother that he needed. Joseph's family would not let him visit his father, so they were never able to say goodbye or make peace with each other. When Joseph was 12, his father died, so the son lost his only source of love and acceptance.

Joseph pushed himself through school and college, to receive an MBA. During his years with large companies, he always felt as if he was not accepted even though he did well. His interpretation of the way people accepted him obscured how they *actually* treated him, for when you have a poor self-image, and low self-esteem and self-worth, you take even a trivial slight as rejection.

He left the corporate world to go into business with a partner but that, too, failed because the partner was basically a crook. In desperation, he quit working and began trying to find himself.

He wandered for several years looking for the answers, until in 1993, he volunteered at a Whole Life Expo. As a room monitor, he was assigned to my lecture room and listened to my presentation. He was so taken with what he heard that he made an appointment with me.

In our sessions, we found many "I want to die" programs that he created at the time of his father's death because he wanted to be with his father. He was also able to see how he had chosen certain people in his life in order to validate how he felt about himself.

When we began to clear his childhood trauma, we ran into more buried programs than I had ever experienced in one person other than myself. We discovered that he had given up and was running on autopilot to the point that his Subconscious Mind had total control of his life; he had not a shred of control over his life, so the first step was to reclaim his power.

However, every time he tried to reclaim his personal power, he fell into illusion and blamed others for the problems in his life. In 1993, I didn't yet know that the Subconscious Mind backs up all its programs each day, and has program regenerators, recreators, and reactivators that will recreate programs. Further, when the incidents are traumatic, the Subconscious Mind covers them up with denial and denial-of-denial, so we have no conscious awareness of them at all.

For many years, we ran around in circles, clearing the same programs over and over. Even after we became aware that the programs were regenerating, some of the same programs continued to come up. This baffled us because we were sure we'd removed and deleted them. We also found that as we cleared the programs in the current files, the programs that were in denial moved forward to replace them. After they were cleared, the denial-of-denial files begin to move forward.

In February 1994, Joseph came to a Neuro/Cellular Reprogramming workshop. This was a breakthrough for me because we could then work together on how this process worked. He asked how he could learn to be clairvoyant, so I taught him how to use a pendulum for dowsing. Whenever he became daunted by the huge body of information, I told him, "You can learn if you are prepared to discipline yourself."

Once he developed his psychic abilities, he was able to release the programs on his own, and astonished himself at how easy it was. This breakthrough validated his self-worth, but even though he had mastered the process, he refused to go into practice and see clients. Many people validated his abilities, yet he was adamant.

Many times, we found the answers to his dilemma, yet he would always retreat into isolation from me so we could not get together to work out his problems. Each time he came back, we had to recover lost ground because he had invited people into his life who had sabotaged his progress.

We discovered that all the women in his life had been controllers whom he had invited in because he wanted to heal the relationship with his mother and be taken care of. In fact, when he was 50, he had moved to the East Coast to try to win her acceptance, but she still treated him as she had in the past.

In 1998, matters came to a head when he finally recognized the pattern. One day, he called me from his home to ask if I would meet him at the Sacramento airport. Like a frightened child, he was running away from the woman he was living with who was dragging him down and controlling him.

Joseph realized that he was letting his programs run his life, even though they were sabotaging his life. One addictive relationship after another supported his need to be taken care of until the level of control threatened to engulf his freedom. He would then escape, only to move in with another woman who would do exactly the same thing.

Oddly, Joseph's marriage didn't work because his wife refused to control him. However, her family did not accept him and eventually succeeded in sabotaging the relationship so he would leave, which he finally did. Joseph has an amazing bond with his son from that marriage that continued after the divorce. His son is very strong and apparently came into this life with a strong sense of self that was unaffected by the examples of his parents. He was open to my work and has had many sessions with me that helped him further develop his self-esteem and self-worth.

Realizing that you've been running away from lessons all your life is hard to deal with. If you've never really felt good about yourself and have never been in good physical health, you don't know what you're missing. As Joseph now says, "I know how it feels to feel good about myself and be in good health, so when I slip back, I really know it now. I didn't know how it felt to feel good in the past as I'd never experienced it and had no frame of reference to measure it against. Now I do know, and I never want to return to the past."

Working with Joseph has been good for me because we've been through many of the same experiences. He's been a good research subject because he has no limitations that would stop us from working together now. In the last two years, we've had many breakthroughs together because we'll work at it until we find the cause.

Now that he understands the N/CR process well, he can work on himself. Clearing all the programs and sub-personalities that were running his life took many hours of concentrated work, but he now knows what it feels to be like a "no limit" person. He recognizes now that he was running in circles, chasing his desire to be taken care of by a mother because he was operating out of a codependent victim pattern. Five years ago, he was mad at me for describing his behavior in this manner, but now that he's out of the loop of the illusion and denial, he can see it himself. He has said, "Now that I don't have to live in survival anymore, I can really begin to enjoy my life and make some strides forward."

He now can accept that people will validate him. His self-image is solid and he doesn't need a mother to take care of him. Since he took back his personal power, he has no fear of being alone. Self-empowerment is the final lesson. When you get this lesson, everyone supports you.

It seems that most people suffer from lack of love and self-worth, and low self-esteem and self-confidence. Few people can love themselves or receive love from others. This stems from the ignorance of parents who get caught up in the idea that they must have children no matter what. Unfortunately, few people in their twenties are capable of dealing with and handling children.

In Frank's case, his parents would have been better off if they'd never had children. They treated their son like dirt under their feet. He was not wanted, nor did he get any support or love during his childhood. His father was a heavy drinker and treated his children as if they were farm animals—not a good foundation for success in life.

Frank is a fighter who needs to prove to the world that he is all right and can succeed against all odds. He is determined to make a life for himself so that he doesn't have to live in poverty and survival, as his parents did.

Of course, the greatest challenge is to overcome his childhood programming, for those programs will win the battle no matter how hard you strive, eventually controlling your behavior unless your will power is so strong that you can overcome them.

Frank succeeded through grade school and college even though he got no support from his family. His father told him repeatedly that he would never amount to anything. Why would a father do that? It's called the lowest common denominator program: "I don't want you to threaten me by becoming better than I am, so I will keep knocking you down until you believe me. When you accept what I say, you will never strive to be better than me."

With Frank, however, it had an opposite reaction. He set out to prove to them that he could break the pattern. He received excellent grades in college and was accepted to dental school, graduating a year earlier than normal. He got married, opened a practice, and did quite well in the beginning, but then the lessons began to pop up. You cannot avoid them unless you have tremendous personal power, and even then, they'll eat away at you until they take over. In Frank's case, they did. Autopilot took over and he actually walked out of any conscious awareness of his life.

Sub-personalities began to run his life, and he says, "I simply can't remember thirty years of my life."

If the lessons get really intense, we will run into the magical child. The Magical Child syndrome is common with high achievers from dysfunctional families as Frank was. The intensity of the lessons finally overwhelmed his mind's ability to handle the pressure of his personal life. He continued to work as a dentist and did quite well until the pressure to run away from the lessons became so great that he "crashed and burned."

He reenacted escaping his parents by running away from his wife, who was a duplicate of his parents. Each time, he would set up the same syndrome: getting established in a dental practice and doing quite well, and then meeting up with someone who would sabotage him so he would have run again.

I met Frank at a Whole Life Expo in San Francisco and, at first, I couldn't recognize that he was running away from himself. He put on a good facade to cover his behavior. A few weeks later, he made the 12-hour drive from his home to see me, impelled to find out why his life was not working. In our first session, I saw why. His mind did not want to give up control so we had a hit-and-miss relationship for next three years. Each time we made some progress, he would retreat again.

When we finally managed to have a few sessions, he saw that his marriage was not working and that he had to get out of it. But that wasn't the main problem. He was deeply afraid of coming into his power and taking control. He was still running away from himself. People would destroy him financially and he'd run rather than confront them. Finally he began to work for other dentists who would also take advantage of him.

As long as Frank was sending out the message that he was willing to let people take advantage of him, they did. He ran from coast to coast to find a location he felt would work, but location had nothing to do with it because he took his programs with him everywhere he went. However, he wasn't able to see that yet either, so the lessons got more intense and closer together. The pressure of avoiding the lessons led to erratic behavior, which I did not want to have to deal with.

The lesson that finally woke him came when he arrived at his dental office to open up and found that the locks had been changed. With the help of some outside investors, he had put over $100,000 worth of equipment into the practice, which the investors wanted back. He tried to run again but got sick, almost dying in the hospital emergency room because his electrolyte levels were so out of balance that he couldn't function. This experience seemed to bring him back to reality.

As a good dentist/perodontist, he never had a problem finding a position, and started working in another dental office. However, the partners became upset with him and asked him to leave because he disagreed with some of their attitudes and ideas.

About six months after our last session, he called me and described his experiences. When next in Phoenix for a Whole Life Expo, I spent time with him and saw that he was making progress. Several lessons were up and he was willing to deal with them.

He had developed Carpel Tunnel Syndrome, a wrist ailment his mind created to get him out of dentistry because he was reacting to the negative feelings and fear that patients have towards dentists. (Dentists have the highest suicide rate of all professions due to patients' negative feelings towards them.) His mind was trying to find another method of control to get him out dentistry and protect him. The condition so affected his hand that he could not perform surgery. The human mind is amazing in its attempts to protect you from whatever it feels is jeopardizing your safety. We cleared that program so that he could work in surgery again, but it returned repeatedly because it had many denial programs behind it that slid forward to take its place.

We also found that everyone has a weak point in the body where programs will cluster. With Frank, it seemed to be his wrists, but now that we have cleared all the programs from this location, he is able to continue working.

The only remaining programs involve his guilt about his past treatment of his children. As a result, he lets them control him. They know it and play it for all it's worth. I assume that will be the next major step on his spiritual journey. A breakthrough will happen soon, as he is getting to the point where he can no longer buy their acceptance. When this happens, they too will take a major step in their growth.

When you get to the point of self-empowerment, you can make things happen that would have sabotaged you in the past. Frank has filed legal action against the dentists who forced him out and he will win a judgment against them. The playing field has been leveled, and he now has the personal power to stand up to his saboteurs. He is setting up four dental offices and is succeeding, as he should have 30 years ago. He has changed his name and is totally shifting his behavior. Success is now within his grasp.

In this final case study, the client has been one of my most ardent supporters, and has helped me more than anyone I have met, except for Paul Solomon and Ronald Beesley. I meet Ken in 1987 when a mutual friend set him up with an appointment when I was in San Diego.

Ken's story is the same as many others whose parents lacked parenting skills. His business was setting up networking groups, similar to Rotary Clubs that refer people to each other for business contacts. He felt he was succeeding and wanted to expand but was blocked. Once we broke through all the blocks that were stopping him, he quickly began to expand, establishing groups all over the country.

When we started working together, he had set up only four such groups, but the more he reclaimed his personal power, the more successful he became. We had sessions together whenever I was in San Diego, and often in between. When he was diagnosed with high blood pressure, in one session, we brought it back to normal. He is an excellent client, and is adept at releasing cellular memory. For example, when he became overly stressed, he turned over his business to his daughter but couldn't let go of control. He worked on it and let go. His wife wanted to join the most exclusive country club in San Diego, but he felt uncomfortable with the "high class" members. Once we restored his self-esteem and self-image, he released his feelings of inadequacy around wealthy people and was able to fit right in.

When I suggested that the spiritual journey is easier when you're on a semi-vegetarian diet, he went for it without hesitation. Surprisingly, Ken had had little contact with spiritual principles before he met me, but eagerly committed himself to the path. The more we cleared, the more he let go of judgment and control, and the more happiness and joy came into his life.

I have been working with Ken for 13 years, and feel that he has made the most progress with the least stress. He exemplifies the "no limit" person." His spiritual journey has led him to peace, happiness, harmony, and joy. Today, Ken has retired and spends considerable time volunteering on projects and continuing with his transformation.

Life is not about hard work and drudgery, but about excitement as each new lesson unfolds. It boils down to this: "Am I willing to be a no-limit person? Do I need validation from others? Am I willing to put myself out there with no concern as to whether people will accept me? And can I maintain my happiness and joy at the same time?"

I enjoy working with people who are willing to take the bull by the horns and run with it. Some people call themselves success coaches; I am a software developer who assists people in rewriting their computer programs. No negative concept or action, illness, disease, or emotional or mental dysfunction exists in the mind/body/spirit without a program or sub-personality in the mind to drive it. Mental computer programs drive all actions and behavior patterns. Positive, no-limit programs cause you to rise to a level of greatness. Negative victim programs cause you to sink and fail. What do you choose in this mystery school of life? The answers are right in front of you if you choose to listen.

6

Connecting With Source

Many people just open to anything that comes along, but it is dangerous to enter the inner planes without a guide. Venturing into channeling without a specific reference point calls for great discernment. Dark force energies from all levels try to get to people and misdirect them, and we need to use all the means at our disposal to ensure we are in contact with only beings of light.

Paul Solomon trained me to always ask, "Who I am in contact with?" and make sure they identify themselves. By Universal Law, when you ask a being to reveal itself, it must do so. I have found that negative beings will depart rather than identify themselves, and the Intergalactic Council has told extraterrestrial dark forces to pull back from planet Earth. However, we must still deal with demonic beings and inter-dimensional beings from the astral plane intent on controlling humans. Being hard to detect, these entities work insidiously.

For safety, it is best to call on a guide to help you across the astral plane. When you are reaching out to a higher being, you must raise your vibration to connect, and cross the fourth dimensional plane, but doing so without protection can be dangerous. Therefore, I always call on my Higher Self and the Holy Spirit to guide me through.

Begin by forming a relationship with your Higher Self. The best way to do this is through meditation and dreams. Your Higher

Self is ready to go on-line any time you indicate your desire, all you need do is communicate your desire and use the proper method. But first, make sure you do not have an inner shadow blocking access. Most people are blocked from their High Self by an inner shadow and from GOD by an overshadow.

Meditation or any form of communication is almost impossible if the doors are blocked. Many people we check have several blocks in the way that must be removed in order to allow clear communication channels. Without clearing the blocks to getting true answers, we will get inaccurate results. Fortunately, you can check for blocks with Kinesiology (muscle testing).

Some people have a hard time meditating. If you have continual mind chatter, quieting your mind will be hard. Your sub-personalities may want to stop you, and you may need to make peace with them to get them to work with you. There are several ways to do this, with many books, tapes, classes and seminars on the subject, such as the tape that goes with this book. My book *Being a Spiritual Being in a Physical Body* gives instructions on how to make friends with your Middle Self (or Ego).

Due to stress and fear, people often separate from their body. Your life can function quite well in this state because the computer in your Subconscious Mind will run basic functions without your help for up to 21 days. For example, people in a coma will occasionally check in with their body to keep it functioning. (A coma is something people may choose to experience freedom by leaving the body if they feel they have no freedom in the body. If they decide to leave permanently, it will die.)

Where are we, then, when we are not in our body? The part of us that walks out is from the conscious, rational, decision-making mind. This control room in your mind needs to have an operator in it at all times, otherwise you are not at the controls and someone else is running your life. Regaining control is simple; use this affirmation:

"Today's date is _____ [month, day and year]. I am _____" [first and last name]. I am in my conscious, rational, decision-making mind."

This will pull you back in your body immediately, but locking you there may take more work if programs or issues are causing you to separate from your body. These can be handled with Neuro/Cellular Reprogramming. (See the description of N/CR in *Your Body Is Talking, Are You Listening?*)

You may also have to test for attached spirit beings hanging on the body. You can use Kinesiology to ask, "Are there are any attached entities on this body?" This specialized information is given in our book *2011: The New Millennium Begins.*

Finally, perform one more test to be sure a client does not have any overshadows blocking the client from GOD or inner-shadows blocking the Higher Self. Using muscle testing, ask, "Is there is an overshadow or an inner-shadow?" If there is, then ask your client to think about loving him or herself. Ask him to think about letting other people be kind and caring, and to accept love from others. If the body tests "weak" or "no," the following affirmation will correct it:

"As the Christ Master Self that I am, love is my responsibility and I accept that now. I am removing all overshadows that block me off from GOD. I am reestablishing the Presence of GOD in my life now. I am removing all inner-shadows that block me from my Higher Self and I am doing that now. I am entitled to peace, happiness, harmony and joy in my life now. I accept that now. I am loving myself and accepting myself, and I am doing that now. I am one hundred percent committed to accepting love in my life, and I am doing that now. I accept love as my responsibility; I am entitled to love and I accept that now. I know I am perfectly all right, perfectly acceptable, and I accept that now. Knowing that love is my responsibility, I accept that now. I am loving myself, and forgiving myself, and I am doing that now."

Clients who were rejected as children may not have a "love program" in their mind's computer. Maybe the mother rejected the child before it was born, as happens with one out of four people. Or perhaps during pregnancy, the mother had difficult emotions, which were projected directly to the child's cellular memory.

Even before it is born, the child's mind and body are recording every feeling the mother has. A mother's thoughts of abortion, even if not acted upon, will cause serious defects in the child's self-esteem and self-worth, as happens in one out of twenty people.

The final blow that destroys all self-worth and self-confidence is a failed abortion attempt. Self-rejection is complete and the person will set up circumstances for continual rejection. (I am very aware of this syndrome because it happened to me as a child.)

If you test for a "love program" and it is absent, you may have to write a new one that overwrites the program that drives the "I am not lovable" core belief. If there are problems with issues in this area of life, the new program may not "take," in which case the rewrite may need to be repeated until the blocks are released. (This process is described in detail in my book *Your Body Is Talking, Are You Listening?*)

7

The Use Of Neuro-Kinesiology (Muscle Testing)

I received my original training in Kinesiology from Dr. Frank Diamond, the originator of Behavioral Kinesiology and, over the last 15 years, I developed it into Neuro-Kinesiology as a process that would allow clients to self-validate what I was picking up even without intuitive or clairvoyant abilities. If we direct the mind to ask the question of the right source, we can access anything.

There are many descriptions of Kinesiology, and practitioners often add a prefix to distinguish their individual process. We use Neuro- because we are asking the body to tap into the programs in the mind. It does this by muscle response via neurological system. In actuality, all muscle testing works in this way, no matter what the prefix. The mind gives its response through a neuro-synaptic reaction. All muscle response is controlled by the mind. When you ask the question, the mind accesses its database and reveals the answer. For example, if you ask about a dietary supplement to see if a client needs it, the mind checks the body and reports back in one of three ways: intuitive projection, neuro-synaptic, or neuro-peptides.

You can get your own answers on many questions by using hand Kinesiology, an easy to use process in which you make a circle by touching the tips of the thumb and one finger of one hand. Then do the same with the other hand but interlock the two circles. Tell yourself, "Give me a yes" and try to pull the circles apart. If you can't, this usually means "yes." If you can pull apart easily, this will usually mean "no." Phrase your questions so they are *yes* and *no* questions.

There are many ways to use muscle testing, but in all of them, clarity is of the utmost importance. Also, you must have correct polarity to get accurate answers. If it is reversed, a "no" will record as a "yes" and vice versa. Use the arm or interlocking fingers to test for this, asking whether the polarity is reversed. The majority of the time we get a "no," which indicates that the polarity is reversed.

To correct this, we can use an ancient Chinese temple ritual for balancing the body before meditation exercises. Put your wrists together at the base of the palms, with your fingers facing forward. Make sure that the "bracelets" (the lines across your wrists and base of your palms) are touching each other. Your wrists must be directly opposite each other, touching at the slight step in the base of your palm.

Then rotate your hands one hundred and eighty degrees, so the fingers are now pointed toward your elbows. Your hands are overlapping your arms, with the fingers pointing toward the elbows, with wrists touching each other, exactly opposite each other. Clasp your fingers over your arms and hold this position for 5 to 10 minutes each morning before you get out of bed. Do not clasp your hands together or let your hands slide up your arms.

Four meridians and acupuncture points, especially the circulation meridian, connect in this exercise, which balances your electromagnetic fields, quadrant energies, meridians, and chakras. It also grounds you at the same time.

You can use your mind's awesome abilities to talk to your own body or even to GOD. You can use any set of muscles that will give you an "up and down" action or an "open/closed" indication. Using fingers, you can hold your thumb and middle finger together and try to pull them apart. Using an arm or a leg, you ask the person to resist your pushing or pulling.

Before you begin, however, you must establish your answering convention. To do this, you mentally ask the client to give you a "yes" and a "no." Most people will signal a "no" with weak or no resistance. "Yes" will be strong resistance. Using the fingers, closed fingers usually means "yes" and weak is "no." With the finger method you can test yourself.

The tester must be clear of Middle Self's control and the need to be right. Many sub-personalities, particularly the Authority and Manipulator, will try to control your use of any divination process. The Authority sub-personality always wants to be right.

Outside forces can also impose controls on the effectiveness of the tester. Many people have a program that gives away their personal power to authority figures. It was a useful program during childhood so that we would obey our parents, but it has no value as an adult.

If testers are driven by a sub-personality or are not clear, their agenda will sabotage the test results and muddy the outcome. To clear testers, have them hold an arm up and test to make sure it resists pressure. Ask them to repeat their first and last name while you exert pressure on the arm, until the arm gets weak and drops. This tests for control by a Control or Authority sub-personality. If a sub-personality is in control, you will not be able to test either one. You may want to wait a few minutes and retest to see if the Middle Self is playing games. If it is, the arm will resist again. Retest again until the arm becomes weak. If the arm doesn't go down at all, then that person cannot function as a tester and get valid results.

If the tester is unable to test clear with muscle testing because the arm will not move, there is either a power struggle with the Middle Self's sub-personalities or an outside force such as an entity or an alien who may have control. If a sub-personality is in control, you can tap on the thymus gland to regress or progress, or take the person's power down so you can retest them. While tapping the thymus gland, you say out loud, "Reduce available power to 30 percent." (The thymus gland is located behind the collarbone just below the V-shaped bone below your neck.) If the problem is with the Middle Self, this should work. Remember to return the client to full power before you finish. If you don't, it could cause problems. (If you are unable to use Kinesiology to get accurate answers, seek out an experienced practitioner in clearing outside forces so that you can get accurate answers.)

In Neuro-Kinesiology, you will use both hands. If you ask a question using only the arm, you will get the belief held in the conscious mind, which may not be accurate. When you begin to do this work, always check to see if the Conscious Mind has a viewpoint different from that of the Subconscious Mind so you can experience the difference. To check the Subconscious Mind, put one hand over the client's solar plexus (third chakra) when testing. This will give the Subconscious Mind's viewpoint on the subject, and is always accurate unless you have outside interference, denial, or denial of denial. Maybe the mind does not want to deal with a traumatic incident, so it drops it into denial to avoid dealing with it again. The incident may also be linked to an autopilot that was running at the time, so when the incident was suppressed, the autopilot also went into denial.

If you choose to use a pendulum, you may run into interference from astral entities, or entities within yourself or the client that can control pendulums without you even knowing it. It will appear that the answers are correct, but other forces control them. Brass pendulums seem to work best because they are heavier. (Many excellent books discuss the use of pendulums and dowsing.) Again, you must establish your yes/no protocol by asking your mind to give you the directions for yes and no. The pendulum is just an extension of your mind, and you are projecting the answer out to the pendulum instead of getting it clairvoyantly or through your intuition.

In Neuro-Kinesiology, we get the information through the client's muscle reaction instead of using our own intuition. Quite often when working with a person, you will get a more accurate answer with muscle testing because you are not filtering it through your mind, which could color the answer.

My book *2011: The New Millennium Begins* gives the process and methods to clear outside attached forces or alien entities. When we have cleared all outside forces, we must reach an understanding with the Middle Self that it is not the Source or the Presence of GOD. Some of the sub-personalities would like to think that they are, so you end up channeling your Middle Self.

When you get Middle Self to understand that you gave your power to it when you were a child due to the need for survival, it will begin to work with you. It may take some talking with it to get it to come around. If it does not want to let go of control, you must take a different approach. It enjoys controlling your life and feels threatened because it has to give up control.

Sub-personalities may interpret letting go as giving up their power, and may need reassurance that they are not losing anything but gaining, because you are reclaiming your personal power. It may glory in the fact that it can manipulate you. If that happens, that sub-personality will need deleting and replacing—a skilled process that takes practice. The following process clears many sub-personalities, but this not a complete list as we frequently find new ones.

Take your power back and make friends with Middle Self.

Before you can change any programs, you must take your power back from Middle Self. You can check for this by using Kinesiology. Ask Middle Self if it will work with you. Until Middle Self agrees, reprogramming will not succeed. And if Middle Self is not working for you, it will not file any affirmations in the Subconscious Mind. If Middle Self is left to run on its own program, it will not give up control since has been appointed as your protector.

Before we start any reprogramming, therefore, we must use these affirmations:

"I recognize now that it is my responsibility to reclaim my personal power. I want you to know, Middle Self, that I am taking my power back now. I am not taking your power. I am only taking back the power that is rightly mine. I know I gave my power to you when I was a child because I could not handle my life very well. I did not realize the consequences it would have. I know I have to take my power back and take responsibility for my life now. I know you did the best you could with the programs you had available at the time. I know that I am the computer operator and the programmer. It is my responsibility to install all the program files now. I thank you for your help."

"I want to you to know, Middle Self , that I have to make friends with you now. I know now that in the past, I felt you were the villain and the enemy. I now realize that is wrong. I know now that you are the file manager and the librarian for my Subconscious Mind. I recognize my mistake now. I am giving myself full permission to forgive myself for any harm and trauma that I may have inflicted on you. I need your help since you are an important part of my team. I am loving you and forgiving you, since I know you did the best you could with the programs you had available. I am loving and forgiving myself. I am installing these programs now."

These two affirmations will rewrite the protocol that Middle Self operates under. It will now cooperate with you and file any program you want them to. The following affirmation releases the sub-personalities:

"As the Christ master self that I am, I recognize that I have to release this ____ [name] sub-personality now. I am asking you, Holographic Mind and Middle Self , to remove this sub-personality from the file. Remove all _____ [exact number] sub-personalities from the Conscious Mind's operating file, from the Middle Self's operating file and from the back-up file. Remove all _____ [number] from the timeline file. Put them in the archives, lock them up, and seal them so they will never affect me again. Delete, erase and destroy all the operating systems, operating programs and operating instructions. Remove all the programs that are supporting and driving these sub-personalities and put them in the archives, too. Delete, erase and destroy all the programs, patterns, records and the operating instructions. Lock all these sub-personalities, patterns, programs, and records in the history section under a control lock so they will never be able to activated or recreated again, and will never be accessible by me or anyone else under any circumstances."

This does not mean that they will never be reinstalled since your Conscious Mind can recreate a new set any time you do not take responsibility to follow through on a decision with action. Do not commit to anything unless you intend to follow through. If you do not follow through, your mind will assume you do not want to move forward on the decision you made. If you do not act, your mind must close that program by creating a sub-personality and a program about not wanting to take action on that subject. If it happens often enough, then an Avoider is installed along with a Not-wanting-to-take-responsibility sub-personality. This can go on indefinitely, and you can become paralyzed by indecision and inaction. If this happens for a number of years, your Instinctual Self will interpret this as if you wanted to die.

Your mind cannot leave any loose ends, and must have closure on every thought, statement or action you take. Even if you start a sentence, it will complete the sentence for you. So every thought and action must be completed or your mind will finish it and file it. It is a good housekeeper, but it may not complete the job as you would have done.

A program creates a sub-personality and will drive it to get the desired result. If self-rejection is carried to the final stage, it will create a life-threatening illness. A dysfunctional program or belief may even create specific disease sub-personalities. A disease, illness or dysfunction cannot exist in the body without a program to drive it. Some activating force must trigger a breakdown of the immune system, or cause stress on the adrenals or the endocrine system.

So, when releasing programs, make sure that you check for the sub-personalities that are enabling them. Each time you clear a time line or operating file, it may activate another series that has been set to be installed from a back up file.

When clearing karmic files, check for gatekeepers and guards that are connected with the files. They will try to block release of the files.

If a person degenerates or sets up "I want to die" programs, the control of the mind/body shifts the Instinctual Mind, which can result in programs being set up in this mind. If there is a conflict in the Instinctual Mind or fear of dying, it will set up fear of dying programs and sub-personalities in the Survival Self (part of the Middle Self). This the main cause of Alzheimer's disease.

When clearing, you must clear all denial and denial-of-denial programs and sub-personalities. Use Kinesiology to ask, "Is this program a belief?" and, "Is this program a reality?" If yes to both, then ask Holographic Mind to go through all the veils, shields and illusions, and reveal the truth. Continued positive response indicates a program locked into the physical body.

If the response to the reality question is weak, we have denial, so ask Holographic Mind to bring up all hidden denial and denial-of-denial programs. Check for them and clear them from all files. Traumatic situations will also have timelines that can be in denial, also. They can also be in autopilot in denial or denial-of-denial.

We must also check for Recreators, Regenerators, and Reactivators that will create the same program again and again. These will be attached to individual programs, so you must check each program for this each time you clear the program and sub-personality.

Five basic sub-personalities are indigenous to the mind and cannot be removed. However, you can remove the programs and the sub-personalities that they created to support themselves. The five sub-personalities are:
- Survival Self
- Instinctual Self
- Inner Child
- Critical Parent
- Inner Adult

The following sub-personalities can be removed and cleared totally:
- Power controller (wants to have power over people, business activities)
- Controller (wants to control everything around it for security)
- Authority (know-it-all)
- Blocker (blacking a person out mentally)
- Manipulator, Justifier, Nobody Cares For Me
- Ingratitude, Avoider, Scaredy Cat, Rebel
- Procrastinator, Projector, Insecurity
- Blamer, Annoyer, Nagger, Resenter, Struggler, I Don't Fit In, I'm Not Accepted, I'm Not All Right, Self-righteous

- Protector, Sufferer, Confuser, Feeling Sorry For Self, Savior, Self-pity, Rescuer, Pulling Sympathy From Others, Saboteur, Indecision

Rejection and abandonment sub-personalities can take many forms:
- People are rejecting what I say
- People are rejecting who I am
- Rejection by mother
- Rejection by father
- Rejection by others
- People do not trust me
- People don't accept me.

Many sub-personalities support anger programs. A few are listed below, and you will find more in the clearing process:
- Anger at having to reach out
- Refusal to reach out
- Anger at moving forward
- Refusal to take responsibility
- Anger at not being accepted.

Fear can take many forms also:
- Fear of being rejected or not accepted
- Fear of reaching out or venturing forward
- Fear of vulnerability
- Fear of having to take responsibility
- Fear being abandoned
- Fear of failure
- Fear of own inadequacy.

When clearing any program, feeling or beliefs in any way, if the Middle Self (file manager) is not working with you or the client, nothing will be filed. Whether or not you thought about Middle Self as the enemy in the past makes no difference. Somehow Middle Self picked up that you saw it as the villain, maybe through something you read or heard someone say. I have yet to find someone who did not consider their Middle Self the enemy.

Very seldom have I found Middle Self working with clients unless they were from a totally functional family, but in 20 years of practice, I have encountered only 5 people from such families.

Before you can begin work with clients, you must check for their love programs and rewrite if missing (see *Your Body Is Talking, Are You Listening?*).

Finally, note that some of the above sub-personalities can affect a client's ability to use any form of muscle testing. This process will be described in more detail in a future book, *Psychoneuroimmunolgy Mind/Body Medicine Connection*

We are now ready to connect with the Akashic Record.

PART THREE

ACCESSING THE AKASHIC

8

What Is The Akashic Record?

The Akashic Record is a database that was set up for you when you decided to enter the physical universe. From your first incarnation on, it records every thought, word, emotion, and action, plus all your lessons and how you handled them. You also record the same information in your subconscious mind and body's cellular memory, along with how you feel about the way you are treated. As the information builds up, you will begin to experience the effects emotionally and physically in your body. Quite often people will mistake the pain that appears as some situation that must be released so they treat the symptom rather than the cause. By avoiding the lesson, it will come up again and again until you take notice. The Record records each time you avoid the lesson and will bring it up with greater force the next time until you finally "get it."

When you decided to descend from a spark of light into the physical universe, you set up a meeting with the Lords of Karma. They relayed to you everything you needed to know about universal law, spiritual principles, and the galaxy you chose to incarnate in. They also set up a database for you in the Akashic Record and told you how it works. You read the instructions and the rest is history.

In its first incarnation, the new soul is fascinated by all the opportunities to experience the physical world. At that time, it is aware of the diversions that would separate itself from the spark of light that it is, but inevitably, Middle Self and Conscious Mind get so caught up in the physical world that they drop further away from GOD Source, and become lost in the physical world.

After many such incarnations of separation, we are now trying to find our way back to who we were when we departed from our original true self. We are trying to heal the separation with Self. However, many people have difficulty in reading the Akashic Record and following the guidelines given to us in the beginning. They let fear enter and get lost again, possibly for lifetimes. The question is, "Is this the lifetime when you are ready to reclaim your true direction?"

The Akashic Record tracks each time you refuse to see the truth and go off on a detour. The Lords of Karma, your guardian angels, guides, teachers, GOD, and your Higher Self have no vested interest in you recognizing where you are. Since there is no time in the soul dimension, you have as many lifetimes as you want to realize that you are the Christ Master Self. The Christ Force is ready to manifest through you as soon as you see the light of love and forgiveness for yourself.

The Lords of Karma explained to you that there are lessons you will have to learn and that you must be careful of the physical desire state you are entering. It has pitfalls that will divert you from the true path. You may get into competition, judgment, need to control, or lose yourself in rejection and emotions. We seem to be lost even though the records are right before us. We let fear and anger divert us from our true path. We try to understand the lesson, but fear seems to drive us away.

Each time we face a lesson, we create a record in our subconscious mind of our response. Each cell in our body is a node in the "computer network" that communicates with the main computer in our Subconscious Mind. This cellular communication is by electrical/chemical reaction, and affects the fascia tissue, the muscles, organ meridians and the acupuncture points. Positive responses on our part are logged in the Akashic Record and your Subconscious Mind, but do not affect the cellular structure of the body. Negative reactions, however, are additionally recorded in the body, and will eventually cause dysfunction in the body and mind.

The Lords of Karma do not edit the karmic records in the Akashic Record; they just maintain them and help you, before each incarnation, to review the lessons you have before you. You choose the lessons you are willing to take on in your new life and the set of parents who will provide you with the imprinting you will need. From then on, you choose how you will handle the lessons.

The Lords of Karma, or any being from the spiritual realm, including GOD, will not intervene in your lessons. However, few of us remember the lessons we chose or how to access the information after we enter the body. The more traumatic the lesson, the less likely we will be able to remember it.

We will continue on the cycle of return until we clear all the lessons that have not been completed. The simplest way to hasten the journey is to get into your Hall of Records and search out all the lessons that have to be completed and begin to work through them. However, reading your own records and getting a clear understanding is difficult, and it's best to have another person read the records with you (provided that person is clear of controlling influences).

The Akashic Record is kept in the fifth-dimensional Hall of Records, and the best way to access this is by active meditation. With the proper technique, you can go to the record-keeper and ask for the books on the lessons you must learn to advance on the path. Because meditation is a personal experience, each person has an individual experience of the Hall of Records.

Each person in your life is your teacher, here with a gift for you, but you must recognize the gift and the lesson. The Akashic Record will help you on the journey, with guidelines for achieving peace, happiness, harmony and joy in your life. The Holographic Mind has all the necessary information, and all you need do is access the records in the soul level of the mind.

You must be willing to accept the lessons and the teacher, who could be your worst enemy. It could be that you have a past life with this person that needs to be completed. It does not have to be accessed in detail; all you need know is the incident and how to rectify it. When you see the lesson clearly, you must let go of judgment, control, authority, anger, fear, and manipulation to release the lesson. What actually happened is history and does not matter; you must let go with love and forgiveness, no matter what or how it happened.

You set up all your lessons and choose the method you will use for learning. You cannot damage anyone, in any way. If you try to take control, extract revenge or let your anger divert you from being helpful, you are just creating more karma and getting farther from your path. If we hurt anyone in any way, even if we are not aware of the action, we have just moved farther off the path into a detour in our life. *The lesson is always about treating everyone with kindness, caring, love and forgiveness, without judgment, in every situation.* There is no need to experience the karmic law of "an eye for an eye," but if we do, we just keep adding to the Akashic Record karma file.

But if we do not read the records and release the karmic lessons, karmic law will prevail, and we will have to learn the lesson whether we want to or not. If we choose the lesson, we will set ourselves up to go through the experience. Would it not be more comfortable to release it with an affirmation than go through the experience with pain and suffering? It is possible; miracles do happen every day. They have in my life; they can in yours, too.

Genetic defects are nothing more than a choice we made to deal with a karmic lesson prior to birth. They manifest as defects or dysfunction in the body after birth. We choose the parents who will provide us with this genetic breakdown so that they can learn a lesson, too. Those lessons can be released and healed if you can get through to the Middle Self, Lower Self and soul, to help the lessons be understood, and let them go. You do not have to communicate with Conscious Mind. You must go directly to the records in the Subconscious Mind and reprogram its computer. Miracles do happen when you let go of the base cause.

Christ Consciousness is in all of us. We just have to recognize it and turn on the switch with love and forgiveness.

9

Accessing The Records

Before meditating, doing clairvoyant or psychic readings where I plan to ask for guidance, communicating with Source, or accessing the collective mind or the Akashic Record, I use the following affirmation to plug in my "phone line" to my higher self and the Highest Source of my being. This carries me past the astral plane and the common astral entities that masquerade as spirit guides in order to misdirect us:

"As the Christ Master Self that I am, I am one hundred percent committed to entering the Highest Source of My Being through my higher self. My higher self, holographic mind, Presence of GOD, Holy Spirit and my guardian angel are guiding me into your presence now. I am in your presence now."

As we have seen, Kinesiology is an effective way to access the records in your cells or Subconscious Mind, since it can give you answers to most any question. Or tune your mind to the Akashic Record and you can ask questions about anything without needing to be psychic or clairvoyant. All it takes is two people who can ask questions properly.

To communicate with records held in the physical body, we use muscle testing, followed by an affirmation to release the beliefs. But to release encrypted or encoded programs, we will need to use Neuro/Cellular Reprogramming (N/CR) (see *Your Body Is Talking, Are You Listening?* for details).

Past life records can be accessed with an affirmation, and then you can use your clairvoyant abilities to read the records. There is no need to use hypnosis to access records if you learn how to use muscle testing with your clairvoyant abilities, and support the release with N/CR. If you use hypnosis in order to see the records directly, you will have to release the programming that you experience. Hypnosis alone will not release the records, patterns and programs.

To release something from a past life, use the following affirmation:

"As the Christ Master Self that I am, I am returning myself to my original incarnation. I am reviewing the records and programs in reference to _____ [fill in subject]. I am bringing the records up to the present time so I can review them and release them now. I am bringing them up to the present moment. I am doing that now."

This will cause the Subconscious Mind's computer to turn on the "VCR" and replay the tape so you can get the information either in pictures or verbal form. However, if you are dealing with a traumatic experience, the Lower Self's sub-personalities may block it. If that happens, go up to the Akashic Record by using the affirmation to access the higher self. Ask the record-keeper to provide you with the record on the subject. As you get an understanding of the record, you can clear it by reciting the following affirmation, which recognizes it as something from the past that is affecting you now. (This requires clairvoyant ability and will take some practice.)

"As the Christ Master Self that I am, I recognize the lesson now. I am claiming Grace and releasing this bondage now. I have already paid the price. I am releasing this lesson now. I have claimed Grace. I am asking my Middle Self to take all the patterns, programs and records out of the file. I am asking you to take all the patterns and programs out, and delete, erase and destroy the operating instructions from the patterns, programs, encoded programs and messages, and lock them up in the archives with the records so they will not affect me again."

We have been accorded Grace by GOD. All we need do is understand the lesson, forgive ourselves, and be able to receive forgiveness from those whom we have hurt or damaged. In this way, we do not have to suffer the effect of the lesson. By claiming Grace, we are stating that we understand the lesson. If we actually have handled the lesson and we claim Grace, the record is filed in the Akashic Record archives and released from the body and subconscious mind. We are thus released from any effects or consequences of the karmic lesson.

You cannot unilaterally decide you have handled a lesson and assume that it is released. You can only fool yourself. Illusion and denial may work for you, but you are not the one who decides if the lesson is cleared. You may be tested to see if you have indeed released your attachment to the lesson. If you have, it will be filed in the archives and your Higher Self will indicate that the lesson is cleared.

Many times, we will be sure that we have handled a lesson, but actually we did not clear it. Your Higher Self and Subconscious Mind are in continual communication with the Akashic Record-keepers, even if you are not aware of it. When they want to get a message to you, you will tune into the filing process while dreaming. The message may be symbolic, so you must to decipher the language of your mind's communication.

As an example of this lesson, in 1982, I was at the Whole Life Expo in San Francisco. A man asked me about the products of an exhibitor at the show. For about 15 minutes, I proceeded to badmouth the exhibitor's products and put him down. I did not like his business practices, but that is all I should have said. I created an immediate karmic lesson about judgment. That night, I woke up with a fierce earache and was unable to sleep due to the pain. The next morning, healers at the show tried to clear it up but nothing worked. The next night, I had an earache in the other ear that finally eased about noon. Obviously, I was not getting the lesson, so my Higher Self instructed my Lower Self to do it again, so I had another earache back in the first ear. The following morning, I was totally deaf and had to cancel all my clients for the next week.

During the week, a client phoned needing help. My wife told the caller that the only way we could do it was for her to write down his end of the conversation so that I could respond. He asked if I was able to ask for a special dispensation because this would take too long. I asked and it was granted, but as soon as I put the phone down, I was deaf again.

Two days later, I realized what the lesson was, and I wrote to the man I had talked with, explaining the situation in detail. I asked him to forgive me for saying what I did, and added that I was forgiving myself for the uncalled-for attack on the exhibitor. I again stated that all I should have said was that I did not like his business practices and should have refrained from attacking him personally or his products. The following week, my hearing started to return. He had obviously received the letter, and the forgiveness from him and myself released the lesson. My hearing took almost a month to heal totally.

I have had many such direct experiences with other lessons. You do not have to contact the person directly as I did, but it does work faster. If you seem to be blocked, you can go through an intermediary, such as a therapist, who knows how to handle situations such as this.

Your Book of Life is filed in the Hall of Records on the fifth dimension, which you can reach through meditation. Your teacher will help you locate the books and read them. As you get comfortable with the process of using the Collective Mind, you can access all the records on demand without the need for meditation. Using your clairvoyant ability, you can go on-line any time you choose.

10

Accessing the Akashic Record

Accessing the Akashic Record requires that we follow a very specific protocol that does not involve using psychic ability. Psychic work uses the third chakra and can be colored by the reader's beliefs and interpretations. Instead, we must use our clairvoyant and clairaudient abilities—our sixth sense abilities. However, the catch is still that clarity is all-important. You must be clear of all outside influences, for they will misdirect your channel to their frequency or information source. You may think you have a clear connection but astral beings are subtle in their control. If you are not using the proper protocol to get past their influence, they can slip in.

Many alien beings have joined with the astral beings to offer their technology to them. For example, the rebel Andromedans are masters at mind control, and can project programs and beliefs into Middle Self, which then accepts them. If you have not made peace with Middle Self so that it works with you, it is open to subtle, covert mind control.

Now, I have heard people say, "I don't believe in dark forces, negative entities, or alien beings, so I don't attract them. If you focus on them, you attract them." I did not believe in them either until 12 years ago when I ran headlong into one. A women came into my bookstore and asked, "Could you please help me? I was driving to work yesterday just like normal, but when I approached a curve in the freeway, I couldn't turn the wheel. It seemed as if the steering column lock had jammed. I finally slammed on the brakes and almost hit the overpass support. It really shook me up. I sat there for about an hour, then I ventured out and everything seemed alright. I talked with one of the psychiatrists at the hospital where I work and he said something must be wrong with my car. That night, I drove home on surface streets, as I was afraid it would happen again. I took the car to the dealer and he found nothing wrong with it. He thought I was nuts because nothing could have done that. I didn't go to work today because I have to get to the bottom of this. I came to your lecture once and you mentioned that there were astral forces that would affect people at times. So I wonder if you can help me?"

I set up an appointment for her later that day. I was wondering what I was going to be up against this time. A new adventure that I had not experienced before with a client. In the session, I went through my normal balancing procedure, and the woman passed out. An entity began to interact with me immediately, using her voice modified to sound male. "What are you doing? I am here to help Shirley. You're not even a Christian. You do not have a Bible in this office. I am not leaving and you cannot get me out."

In response to the Bible statement, I picked up a Bible and put it in her hand. At that point, I knew I was up against something that I'd never experienced before. Concerned for the client, I called in two other therapists to help me. After a major effort, we managed to remove the entity. This was my first entry in dealing with discarnate possessive beings, and seemed to put up a red flag that attracted them. People started coming to me with bizarre stories about their encounters. However, you can choose to live on autopilot, believing that, "Ignorance is bliss."

Many people claim to be connected to the Highest Source or to GOD, yet you can see by the information they bring in that some negative source is influencing them, albeit subtly. Too many people have made predictions only to find that they did not happen. Why? They didn't get past the astral beings in the fourth dimension. Use the affirmation in Chapter 9 to go past them before going into meditation or accessing the Akashic Record.

Another problem with predictions is that they cannot be laid in stone. Every moment, the individuals making up humanity are evolving or devolving, and any information we receive can shift from hour to hour.

Paul Solomon taught us to consistently follow a specific protocol to achieve our goal, beginning with the desire and determination to take responsibility and follow through. Commitment is vital because you are dealing with a "computer" in your Conscious Mind, and a Middle Self that will step in and take over if you go on autopilot. If you are not consistent in your endeavors, your Conscious Mind will assume that you do not mean real business. But if your Middle Self and your Conscious mind take over, they will not be as willing to work with you the next time you attempt to get on the path.

You could, in fact, get into a battle of the "Dark Night of the Soul" because your teacher from the White Brotherhood will set up lessons for you and bring people into your life to work those lessons out with. The fact that you have free choice as to whether or not to take the path is true up to a point. Once you embark on a spiritual journey, there is no turning back. You can take detours, but you must always return to the path. Once you make the commitment to follow the spiritual path, your free will to turn back is denied.

I want to emphasize that your detours could last several lifetimes, for your teachers are not concerned with time. They see the big picture, not just one lifetime, and know that eventually, you will make the transition from the third dimension to the fifth. (Contrary to some metaphysical teachers' illusions, there is no "quick fix" that will avoid hard work and discipline.)

The Mystery School of Spiritual Discipline teaches a very specific course that involves a special diet for transfiguration, and attunement to the Presence of GOD through meditation and prayer. The hardest part of this path is letting go of all the sub-personalities that operate out of fear and anger, and cause disorganization, procrastination, and relaxation into autopilot mode. Before you can make this dimensional transition, you must heal your body and release the denials that control your life, as described in my books *2011: The New Millennium Begins* and *Journey Into The Light*.

The more disciplined and committed you become to the path of transmutation and transfiguration, the lighter your body becomes as you move to higher frequencies. Making contact with the Akashic Record is immediate and accurate. GOD Source cannot lower their vibration to come down to us so, to contact them, we must become lighter and move up to their higher vibration.

I discovered that I could live in a duality and move between dimensions to make contact easier, but it can throw you out of sync at times. I have found that as I released most of my third-dimensional habit patterns, I was able to live in a higher dimension, yet still function in the third dimension. When you drop all the anger and fear programs that control your behavior, moving between dimensions becomes easy.

Part Four gives a framework that you can use to set up a spiritual path that you can follow. My book *Being A Spiritual Being In a Physical Body* is an adjunct to this book. I have also found that *A Course In Miracles* can help shape the path, too.

PART FOUR

THE PATH

11

The Meditation Process

Many cultures, societies, and organizations teach meditation. To some, it is the *only* thing you need do to reach enlightenment. My experience suggests otherwise, yet it is an important ingredient in the process, and it will raise your vibratory level thereby allowing enlightenment to happen. Some people devote three to five hours a day to meditation; in my opinion, your time could be better used serving planetary enlightenment.

According to GOD Source, sitting on a mountaintop or in silence by yourself, contemplating what you could do, does very little to change the planetary energy and consciousness. Actively taking part in groups working together is more powerful and seems to be more valuable.

I agree that one should meditate daily, but that it should be limited to 30 to 45 minutes, even shorter if you practice two or three times a day. I also believe it should be active meditation with a dialogue with your Source. My experience suggests that passive meditation separates you from your body. *On the other hand it is very important to be able to leave your body in process of meditation so that you can have a clear channel. Getting a clear channel is a real challenge.*

To ensure a clear channel, you must move beyond the astral plane, with its dark forces of interdimensional and demonic realms where, for thousands of years, dark forces from alien societies have masqueraded as masters of the light. Coming from highly developed technological races, these aliens can give you advanced information but it is laced with mind control. They are looking for unsuspecting humans who will open up to their dialogue. They would love to control people who are looking for an ascended being to communicate with. Not all souls that are out-of-body are ascended beings. Many earthbound souls have been hooked by the dark forces, and got caught up in the power given them by unsuspecting individuals. Many beings are waiting for you to give them your life direction and control. So to contact Sources that are not connected with dark forces, you must move to the fifth dimension or above.

To communicate with an ascended master, you are nearing that level of enlightenment yourself. Many years ago, Paul Solomon said that in his experience, less than 2 percent of those who claim they are communicating with ascended masters are actually doing so. He asserted that if you are talking with an ascended master, you are close to mastership yourself. Again, people can delude themselves into thinking that they are communicating with an ascended master so they must be approaching mastership. This is, of course, coming to an invalid conclusion by making assumptions that one validates the other. Both are denials of the illusion. (My book *Journey into the Light* describes how to evaluate where you are in your enlightenment process.)

Meditation is a powerful tool if used properly, but understand that closing your eyes and quieting the body is not meditation but simple relaxation that does not stop the incessant chatter in your mind. Being able to master the self-chatter is the first step. Then, you can begin to contact your Higher Self, and then your Source. Eventually, you will be in intimate contact with your Source Self at all times. To do this, you must use visual imagery to build a separate reality outside of yourself that can become so real that you may want to stay in that other reality. The challenge is live in both worlds at the same time.

Meditation is a beginning, not an end. For me, it was a great beginning because it allowed me to communicate at any level I chose. It is an attunement process, and the more you align with Source and listen to the lessons each day, the more you will become anchored in your body.

Ronald Beesley, a teacher under whom I studied in the 1970s, said, "Meditation is not to remove you from your body but to connect you more solidly to your body. You came to this planet to work on lessons in enlightenment because you cannot get them on the spiritual plane. Life is a workshop and you came here to work, play, and to have fun. It is not a drudge unless you view it that way. You must live with your feet on the ground and your head in the clouds."

Beesley is saying that we must be aware of where we are at all times. We are the computer programmers and must direct the course of our life.

My feeling is that meditation is an attunement to be able to "pick up the phone" to GOD Source. It is a process to get direct information on where we are and how to direct our life. It works best when coupled with the journal process (see Chapter 15 on the journal process).

Meditation is a discipline, and like all disciplines, you must follow it consistently and rigorously, or your mind will assume you are not committed.

12

Building A Separate Reality
(An Outline for a Meditation)

There are many realities over and above the physical reality with which we are familiar. If you create and explore a separate reality, you will become aware that you have five more subtle senses that parallel your physical senses. The latter are limited to your immediate location, but with the new senses, you can see beyond your current time-space into a new world that is much larger than the physical world. You will be able to see, hear and feel in the alternate reality. The more you repeat the process, the more familiar it becomes.

There is a greater mind that has more wisdom and knowledge than we do. This greater creative mind can impart knowledge to us that can help us live our lives more effectively. Our mind is a part of this creative mind since the presence of GOD is within us; we only need to turn it on and become more familiar with it. Through the use of our more subtle senses, we can become more connected with the Highest Source of Our Being. Your inner teacher can impart information to you through a separate reality where you are open to new material because the physical plane is not blocking perception. There is no limitation in this reality.

The point is not to go into a "no-space," but into a separate reality that evolves so clearly that it becomes a place where you go when you want to communicate with your Source or teacher.

To reach this point of departure, we use guided imagery to separate from the physical and then move to the alternate reality. At this point, we are ready to shift into meditation. To make this point of departure, all voice input from physical reality must stop or it will hold you from making the shift into true meditation. You can play soft music but nothing else should distract you during this shift into meditation and total immersion in the meditation experience.

The first step in letting go of physical reality is to build a separate reality as your sanctuary, such as a beautiful meadow. It is a place to start, a jumping-off point. By using affirmations and colors to evoke a dimensional change, we use visual imagery to create the break with reality. To begin this process, relax the body using the stretching and breathing exercises described in the next two chapters.

To move into the process, we must practice the visual imagery to step out of physical reality. The more we become familiar with the process, the more we can see, feel, hear, and taste with our subtler senses. As we prepare our mind and awaken the senses of the alternative reality, we draw closer to be able to connect with our teacher.

13

Balanced Relaxation

The following material is taken from training at the Inner Light Consciousness Center, taught by Paul Solomon in Virginia Beach, VA, and reproduced with permission. The author considers the exercises and instructions important in achieving the maximum benefit from meditation.

Step 1: Preparation

Begin your meditation experience with a review of your purpose for entering the experience. This is your best protection in any psychic or spiritual experience. If it is to satisfy curiosity or to acquire power over others, you will be unprotected. If, however, your purpose is to achieve perfect harmony with the Creative Force of this universe, your purpose protects you. The very act of reviewing your purpose and ascertaining its compliance with Divine will is in itself a prayer of protection.

Step 2: General Relaxation

We concern ourselves with relaxation in a meditative or spiritual experience because we are seeking a "non-sensory" or "nonphysical" experience. The body, its appetites, and sensory voices can be a distraction in reaching that most effective state. Balanced Relaxation serves the purpose of setting the body aside for a spiritual experience, making it a tool rather than a hindrance.

Step 3: Differential Relaxation

If we compare tension with relaxation to establish a point of reference for ideal relaxation, we can become more thoroughly relaxed. There is a deceptive kind of tension known as "residual tension" that often remains when we feel as if we are perfectly relaxed. This residual tension can distract us and bring us sharply back to awareness of the physical when we wish to work with our new set of senses. "Differential Relaxation" will help us seek out and remove these hidden tensions through exaggerating the difference between tension and relaxation.

Step 4: Wash in Christ's Light

"Differential Relaxation" represents the removal and elimination of tension. The washing in Light represents renewal and regeneration, the positive replacement of vital energy. We use the Light of the Christ because it is a healing presence. In this instance, we speak of Christ as "that which is born of God," rather than a figure in a particular religion.

Step 5: Be Still and Know

This fifth and final phase of Balanced Relaxation is the key to the control of all that is in your environment. Practice and belief in this exercise will awaken and develop the ability within yourself to control your destiny. As we sit perfectly relaxed, we may, from time-to-time, feel a twitch, a jerk, an itch, a point of tension that would seem to be an expression of the physical body crying out for recognition and attention. Here we apply the technique of the Master Christ by allowing the body to communicate to us. We then ask it to let go of the tension with a differential relaxation process if needed. If the Middle Self is causing the discomfort from some belief or fear, we must communicate to it that we are not trying to destroy it. All situations that come up must be addressed with forgiveness and love. Reacting in anger or fear will actually cause the situation to continue. Look at each incidence as a lesson to gain more personal power and control over your body/mind.

14

Forms of Meditation Experiences: Moving Meditations, Energy Evocations and Light Breathing

Begin this experience by deciding exactly what it is you want to accomplish and what benefits you want to receive. Then offer a prayer of attunement incorporating your purpose. Remember throughout this experience to inhale through the nose and exhale through the mouth. You may wish to keep your eyes closed during some of the exercises to aid in your attunement. The exercises are in three parts: moving meditations, energy evocations, and light breathing.

Prepare the body for meditation by taking care of the needs of the physical so that it can become stilled and receptive.

Part 1: Moving Meditations

PURPOSE: Incorporates visual imagery and a worshipful attitude to help prepare the mind and body for meditation; stimulates every part of the body; increases circulation; reverses the blood flow; removes toxins.

1. Salutation to the Light of the One

a. Enter attitude of worship with palms together in front of chest and fingers pointed upward in prayer position. Create an atmosphere of Light. With hands together in prayer attitude, slowly raise them above the head.
b. Arch your body backward. Open to the Light, spreading your hands in a semicircular motion.
c. Take in the Light, clasping it to your chest, and bending forward at the waist.
d. Place hands, then the head on the floor, and wait until you feel the blood flow reversed.
e. Bend the knees to kneel, rock back into a prostrate position. Rest and worship.

f. Left foot back, look up to the Light, arching back, and bathe in the Light.
g. Return to prostrate worship.
h. Place right foot back, arching the back. Bathe in the Light.

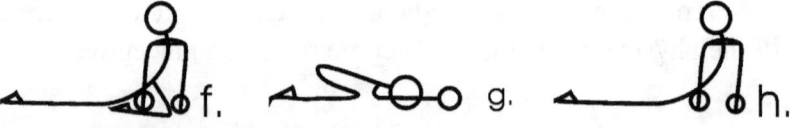

i. Return to prostrate worship.
j. Place both feet back, swing forward as low to the ground as possible, arching the back and swinging up into the cobra.
k. Return to prostrate worship. Kneel. Then stand in the Light, head bowed.
l. Open to the Light.

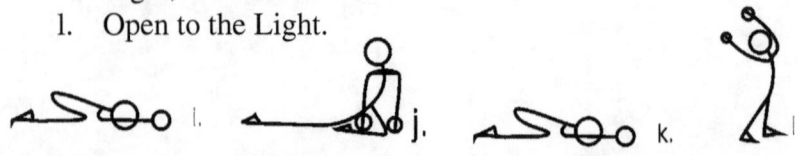

Part 2: Energy Evocations

PURPOSE: Cleanses the body of toxins; increases energy and oxygen supply; feeds the brain; rejuvenates the body, preparing it for meditation.

1. Climbing to the Light (3 times)

    a. Visualize toxins, imbalance, guilt and limitations that need to be expelled from the system. Drop to a crouch, exhaling, expelling impurities.
    b. Open to the light. Reach up as though climbing a ladder and grasp for the Light with the left hand. Bend the right knee by raising the heel while leaving the toes on the floor. Inhale as you stretch.
    c. Alternate raising the right and left leg in a climbing movement four times, inhaling and stretching, and drop again, expelling impurities.

2. Sun Dance Stretch (5 times)

PURPOSE: Focuses on one lung at a time so that each is more thoroughly cleansed.
    a. Crouch to the floor, expelling all toxins.
    b. Slide the left hand down the left leg while arching the right hand over your head.
    c. Drop to a crouched position, exhaling all toxins. Repeat in the opposite direction.

Part 3: Worshipping the Light (3 times)

PURPOSE: Cleanses and fills air in upper air sacs.
  a. Raise hands to the Light and exhale.
  b. With arms extended, bend at the waist to touch your fingertips to the floor
  c. Exhale coming up, hands extended above the head to the Light.

Silent Meditation Active Form

We have an audiotape of guided imagery using the following steps to help you enter this separate reality. To learn the process, it is helpful to use a tape with the guided imagery. (See Appendix D.) Features of the taped process are:

A. *Expectancy:*
  - If you expect change, it will occur, so take it for granted. Expectancy makes meditation dynamic.

B. *Death and Forgiveness:*
  - At death, all of your values move to a higher dimension. Then you evaluate your life, and decide to return to life to put your evaluation to work.

C. *New Life:*
  - You evaluate your life so far, allow the old self to "die" or end the way you see yourself, and then give birth to a new consciousness.

D. *Begin a New Relationship:*
- You become the result of the cause factor called the Teacher. He helps you recognize mistakes, makes you want to change, and causes the change.
- Nature of Teacher: If you are religious, your Teacher is Christ as the Son, born of God, living in you. If you are metaphysical or scientific, your Teacher is the agent of change that functions best as a loving friend.
- Establish a relationship with your Teacher, so that it feels as if someone is there. Use prayer to establish relationship, and look for evidence in life's events.

E. *God's will for me:*
- God's will is what's best for me, as in the prayer: "Help me to release all my wishes and wants and accept now exactly what most suits my needs and opportunities. Thy will be done now, in me and through me."

F. *Taking responsibility:*
- All abilities are now freely available to you, but do you want the responsibility? Can you handle the responsibility? Use the affirmation: "I will receive as much as I can take responsibility for."

G. *The result - The Seventh Garden:*
- Previous six changes were causes; the seventh change is the result of the first six.

H. *Affirmations:*
- *First Level Garden–Red*: "I approach the meditation experience with a sense of anticipation and expectancy. I expect to be changed by this experience."
- *Second Level Garden–Orange*: "I forgive myself all mistakes and errors. I affirm that it is all right to make mistakes. I am not my past. I do not cling to an old self-image. I am prepared to see myself in a new way. I die to who I used to be, and find out who I can become."
- *Third Level Garden–Yellow*: "Old things are passed away, behold all things have become new."

- *Fourth Level Garden–Green*: "I commit myself to increased awareness that I am not alone. There is a 'presence' or a factor alive within me that spurs me on to growth. There is a living impulse to be more than an animal or a machine. This Presence is my teacher, my friend, closer than a brother. I stop all else for a moment to become more aware of this Presence and come to know It better."
- *Fifth Level Garden–Blue*: "Thy will be done."
- *Sixth Level Garden–Violet*: "Because I am now asking for strength, renewal, and inspiration, I commit myself to taking responsibility for all that I receive."
- *Seventh Level Garden–White*: "I commit myself to the silence."

I. Changes in:
- Consciousness
- Attitude
- Thoughts

The Many Facets of the Mantra

Mantrum meditation is using a word, chant, symbol, or a sound that will cause the shift. A *mantrum* is a word, phrase, syllable, sound or vibration which, when repeated, causes a physiological change, bringing relaxation and slowing of body processes. If repeated often enough, it becomes programmed in the subconscious and returns to the conscious mind unbidden, so its use eventually becomes so automatic that you can use it even without conscious effort.

A mantrum is also a trigger mechanism that produces an associated response. So, for example, if you associate your mantrum with peace every time you use it, whenever you do use it, feelings of peace well up automatically and instantly. It becomes a trigger to produce any result you care to associate with it and deliberately produce when you are using it. If you use it to perfect your meditation experience, it will become associated with the meditation experience and with attunement to GOD within you.

The mantrum focuses the mind on a single point, eliminating extraneous thoughts, so when your mind is filled with your mantrum, you can't be thinking about dirty dishes, what you did yesterday, and what you will do tomorrow. When other thoughts come, you can let them pass gently by and return to listening to your mantrum. (20 minutes is necessary for the perfect experience of this phase!)

A mantrum is essentially a mechanical device that opens the aura and the consciousness to a psychically sensitive and receptive awareness. If it is purely mechanical, we are opening in a nondiscriminatory manner, and will open equally to negative thoughts and energies and ideas. However, if the mantrum were a name of GOD, then we are opening exclusively to Higher Presence. Thus, the name of GOD, used as a mantrum, becomes a technique of protection.

A mantrum can direct the consciousness to form a telepathic rapport. If I used your name as a mantrum for a period of time, you would likely respond by calling me, or at least you would find yourself thinking about me without knowing why. I would have extended a telepathic contact. So, using GOD's name as a mantrum will call their attention to me. "Call My Name and I will answer thee and show thee great and mighty things thou knowest not." (Jeremiah 33:3)

It is not possible to call a word or name in meditation without drawing your own thoughts, attention, and energy to the name or concept. So, calling on the name of GOD will focus your mind on them, thus establishing a two-way link with Higher Consciousness.

(We have a set of audiotapes available to help you understand the process and guide you through the steps in creating a meadow and the various forms of guided imagery. It will help you set up the meditation process so you can access the Hall of Records and the Akashic Record and set up the protocol for active meditation to communicate with the GOD Source. These tapes may be available at your local bookstore or from Personal Transformation Press. See Appendix D.)

15

The Journal Technique

This chapter offers a technique that will make a dynamic change and transform your life, if you choose to listen and watch for the lessons being presented to you each day and record them.

Introduction to the Journal Process

The Journal is a useful tool to track your lifecycles and record the lessons that come to you each day. In this way, you can record the progress with your lessons. It is extremely important to know where you are in your path. The Journal will give you some guidelines to follow.

Time on setting up your journal will prove well spent. Place seven 3-ring binder dividers in a binder and label them with the following seven headings. Then add blank paper in each section.

The journal is divided up into the following sections:
1. Daily Entry
2. Dialogue
3. Dream Log
4. Inner Wisdom (listening)
5. Stepping Stones (minor initiations)
6. Discovery (history of your life)
7. Turning Points (major initiations).

Carry with you each day a small notebook to record brief notes of each incident in your daily life that feels as if it may have an impact on you. Each night, enter the information in this section. The Dialogue section has many parts to it that you can use either daily or when the moment seems to signal a need for dialogue with yourself.

The Dream Log is to record your dreams and the direction you are getting from them; the Inner Wisdom section records the revelations you receive, twilight imagery, intuitive feedback, dialogue in meditation, and direct contact with your Source.

Stepping Stones are the minor initiations that you're working on between the Turning Points, such as the temptations you experience, and how you are dealing with them. The Discovery section is your past history, the raw material of your life, lifecycles up this point in your life, turning points in the past; the crossroads and the forks in the road.

The Turning Points are the twelve doors to ascension, your experience at the time you open the door and how you handled the temptations in your progress.

Merely by beginning this process, the lessons will come, seemingly automatically. However, you can control how they progress and their speed. Recognizing the lessons and the potential initiations as they come up is vital. You may be ready to open the door but your Middle Self can create enough fear to block you. You can become victimized by a lesson if you do not have the format and parameters to understand it. Agreeing or disagreeing with the event is not important; the most important part is that you're aware of the situation and can hear and see it without judgment. If you try to justify or go into fight or flight, you lose the lesson and it will recur at another time.

The main function of the journal process is to remind you that you have already been through this before, so that you will recognize the lesson next time. It will also allow you to see the value of what comes to each day. If you can evaluate the cause and process it immediately, you won't internalize, stuff or repress the emotion. If you do not get it right away, at least you will set yourself up so that it will not happen again. Releasing the lesson after the fact is better than not recognizing it at all.

Unfortunately, when you don't catch it the first time, it will get more intense the next time. It seems to double in intensity each time, so the fourth time will be 16 times more intense than the first. With the journal process, you can review your progress and get the lesson by knowing what to look for next time. Your journal will be only as effective and useful as your commitment to being alert to the interactions that happen to you.

The intent is to grow into 24-hour consciousness, becoming aware of everything that is happening at all times, and to rewrite your life script, including dreams. In this way, you can change the outcomes and probabilities for the future. Contrary to some people's interpretations, the future is not locked in. If you know it, you can change it. There are no limitations for the possible human. As you begin your journey through the initiations, you will find that miracles do happen. Keep track of the miracles in your life; they are the win/win situations.

This will be your track to the spiritual journey. The more attention you place on each disruption or procrastination and refusal to take responsibility for an action, the sooner you will arrive at your goal.

1. Daily Log Section

The Journal section is made up of two subsections:
1. *Captain's Log*, a daily entry for all the interactions during the day that records only the actual interaction, with no evaluation.
2. *Validation of Self-Worth*, or how you reacted or responded to the temptations and lessons presented to you each day, an evaluation of your understanding of the lesson, the value you gave the experience, and whether you appreciate and validate yourself.

1(a) Captain's Log

For this journal section, carry a small notepad with you at all times. Life is never dull when you're alert, for nothing happens by accident and no one ever enters your sphere of existence without purpose. The "Captain's Log" is the opportunity to make *brief* notations of the day's experiences to be used with the journal work and the evening's meditation.

The name clues you to how it works. It helps to view your life as a journey on "space ship Earth" and note the occurrences in your life that would be reported in a Captain's Log. The routine occurrences are only recorded by mention. For example, a captain might enter:

"*Jan. 6*: We had just completed our meeting with the crew when …"

The "when" actually constitutes the entry. The ordinary events provide the setting, but the unexpected or meaningful occurrences are the recorded events. Do not wait for an outstanding event to make an entry in the Captain's Log; neither should you waste time and energy filling journal pages about mundane events. Keep your entries brief: just the "who, what, when and how." This section is a running account of the setting in which the incidents of your life occur. These incidents must be examined for meaning and purpose, for accurate and misdirected reactions and, most of all, for lessons contained in your reaction/response to the situation.

EXAMPLES:

Jan 6, 7:09 am: Was on my way to the airport, traffic was heavy and I was in a hurry. A traffic light was flashing red—took 15 minutes extra to get through the intersection. Because it was later in the day, the freeway was jammed and I missed my flight. I experienced great anxiety because I had to reschedule my meetings. I recognized fear and frustration, a loss of control and feeling of being a victim. My stomach and nerves suffered from the anxiety. My whole day was affected.

Jan 7, 9:00 am: Due to freeway accident, arrived at work 30 minutes late. I hoped no one would notice. I tried to look unruffled.

I was sure my anxiety showed. No one said anything. Took all morning to relax.

4:05 pm: Uneventful day at work, so I meditated for 5 minutes before driving home. It is pleasant to feel high and start home feeling good. I was able to resist getting angry with other drivers.

Jan 8, 7:00 am: Woke up feeling really good, yet everyone was upset, which threw me off.

12:30 pm: Tried to set up lunch with my girlfriend. She said I was not considerate of her time and needs, and turned me down. I felt rejected and alone.

3:30 pm: Got to my appointment but Jim no-showed. I'd prepared and was angry but chose not to give my power away to him. It's Jim's problem, not mine. Readjusted my plans and went on my way. Noticed that I was able to detach from the anger.

Some days may contain more entries than this but some may not. It is vitally important to make an entry every day. What doesn't seem important right now may be meaningful later. Every time a feeling, sensation, fear, anger, or any other emotion surfaces, or something catches your attention, write it down. Keep track of everything, and you will be amazed how quickly the lessons come.

You will not repeat many lessons when you stay up with each incident that happens in your life. It's important to list the wins and times when you feel good about what happens. This will validate your progress. Each day before you go to bed, transfer your notes from your notebook to your journal in the appropriate section. As you get into the format, you will notice that you become aware of the lessons as they arise. When you can spot or recognize the lesson immediately, it will be defused and will not affect your body.

1(b) Validation of Self-Worth

If you are searching for greater meaning in relationships and communication, this section is one of the most important of your journal. Understanding cause-and-effect in your interactions with other people can change your entire life path.

You must recognize the meta-communication that you send out, for people will react to your subconscious projection of who you are, even before you say anything. If you can change the unspoken communication, people will respond to you completely differently. If you can understand how you project yourself, you can release the need for facades, fronts, masks, games and covers. We are living in illusion and denial if we think they work, for many people can recognize the facade or mask you are putting up. For example, you may wonder why you were dismissed by someone when you felt you made a good impression. If you will be honest with yourself, this process will reveal to you exactly how you sabotage your efforts.

No one "accidentally" comes into your life, so everything is there by design and your invitation *at some level*. Suppose you notice a person and make an observation. Does that observation trigger judgment, jealousy, surprise, or embarrassment, or does it motivate you in some way or teach you something?

Depending on your mind's programming, every observation will cause either a negative reaction or positive response. This is a way to recognize autopilot reactions. It will also help you realize how you validate or invalidate yourself. If you are honest with yourself and evaluate each situation without denial, you can break through all the illusions in your life. If you do not recognize the illusion, the denial continues. If a person points something out to you, you need to evaluate rather than justify, for the latter always indicates denial.

All rightness is a quality you learn when you detach from the need for outside validation. You cannot find self-esteem, self-worth, self-confidence, and self-love until you self-validate that you are all right under all situations.

If you can recognize that everything is in your life for a purpose, you can change your life path into happiness, joy, inner peace, and harmony. When you begin to recognize the value of others, you will be appreciated more than you ever dreamed possible. You are never a victim unless you choose to be. If you so choose, then everyone will seem to discount or put you down. The challenge is to recognize your all rightness and people will respond supportively. Nobody can reject you except you. You have to buy into their game and give away your power to become victimized.

Start by observing the people close to you in your life and honestly evaluating how you respond to them. For each one, note how this person affects you. Look at the situations and incidents in which you have engaged with them. As you get more familiar with this section, you will able to make instant evaluations. Try to find key words that describe the situation, then make a short entry.

This section is designed to instill a new appreciation for the cast of characters in your life. If you do not like the actors and actresses in your play, you can change them. But, you must first recognize the lessons they bring you. You and your inner plane teacher, who knows what you need to learn, carefully chose them. Evaluate the situation as it happened, with as little emotion as possible. As you work with this section, you will able to evaluate from an objective observer's standpoint.

Here are some guidelines to make this section work for you:
1. Validate the person and not the incident.
2. Appreciate the value of the person and do not enter the negative.
3. Do not consider what you think you *should* feel or how you *should* have responded. Do not put *shoulds* on yourself. Work from your feelings.
4. Always appreciate your value in the situation. Even if your response is negative, find something positive and meaningful about yourself.
5. To change your reaction and correct your faults, you must see some value in yourself. You will make more progress when you are aware of your own value.
6. Do not leave yourself with feelings of guilt or lack of self-worth.

7. If you can recognize the lesson and the temptation next time, you may not fall into the trap.
8. You must be able to evaluate the incident honestly and without denial. It may be a challenge to enter a description of your value in each situation. Was I of value? Did I help those I have validated? Did I do what I could do to help the situation? Did I validate myself? Did I show appreciation for myself in understanding the lesson presented?

The only way this section will work is by being totally honest with yourself and recognizing any denials and illusions.

EXAMPLES:
Person: Boss/Challenger, motivating, demanding, controlling
Spouse: Clings, codependent
Friend: Seems to put me down all the time
Mentor: One-ups me all the time, acts superior.

- *Incident:* Boss challenged me by snapping at me. Embarrassed me in front of others.
- *Worth:* Made me deal with my victim/self-pity. He seems to be unfeeling in his criticism. I guess I have missed this lesson numerous times.
- *Self-validation:* I now see that I can present myself in a more effective manner. To be more effective, I must become a self-actualized person in my life.

- *Incident:* Friend put me down because I was complaining. Made me angry.
- *Worth:* Called my attention to the fact I was running on autopilot.
- *Self-validation:* The putdown was my interpretation. I needed to hear it but reacted as a victim. I can detach and respond more effectively next time.

- *Incident:* Daughter does not want to communicate with me. Has shut me out her life.
- *Worth:* I recognize I was feeling guilty, rejected and was attached to her.
- *Self-validation:* I am releasing my guilt. I did the best I could at the time in bringing her up; I can't control her. I am all right myself and the situation can be resolved by releasing her.

- *Incident:* Driver in car cut me off and almost caused a crash.
- *Worth:* Brought up my anger. I recognized I could not control situation. Autopilot again. Testing my patience.
- *Self-validation:* I automatically get angry when I lose control. Am going to detach myself from situations that I have no control over. I know I can function without getting fired up.

- *Incident:* Mentor tried to one-up me again. He always has a story that's more dramatic than mine.
- *Worth:* Brings up my anger. I was unaware of my complaining and victim attitude.
- *Self-valuation:* I see that I'm trying to get validation from outside. If I describe my situation as a challenge rather than self-pity, people would be more supportive.

2. Dialogue Section

You may find you will use this section daily, but it is not required. This section is for your letters and dialogues with various people, sub-personalities, events, etc. It's best to sort issues out in your mind with *dialogues* before you confront or state your opinion publicly. Rehearsing your dialogue may avoid making mistakes. Dialogues may fall into the following categories:

- *Dear Master letter*, to communicate with your teacher and Presence of GOD.
- *Dialogues with other people*, to air your feelings about issues with the people in your life.
- *Dialogues with your job*, to air your feelings or pat yourself on the back.
- *Dialogues with society*, to express your feelings over societal issues.
- *Dialogues with events* help you learn how to clearly communicate about them prior to engaging in debate with other people.
- *Dialogues with your body*, in which you ask it questions. You may be surprised at the answers you get.
- *Dialogues with sub-personalities*. Use your dominant hand (right if you are right-handed) to talk with your Inner Critic or your Critical Parent, and any sub-personality that is controlled by the Middle Self. Use your other hand to communicate with the selves that come through the right brain, such as Inner Self, Inner Child, Inner Teacher. You can also dialogue verbally.

Let's take a more detailed look at each type of dialogue.

Dear Master Letter

Since your life is carefully arranged to meet the lessons you need, it is a good idea to assume that a Master Teacher (i.e., the Presence of GOD) is at work in your life, arranging the lessons and people in your daily activities. Nothing and no one comes into your life by happenstance. Your Inner Teacher, Higher Self and Master Teacher have arranged every detail.

With this many beings watching over you, you have considerable help available, and all you need do is ask. However, you must be specific and clear, because they will honor your wishes to the letter. Remember, every word you say or think is a prayer and instruction to them to carry out an action in your life.

This superior intelligence helped you to structure your body and lessons to this point. The presence of GOD is with you at all times when you open the door. They would like to have direct communication with you so they can give you the opportunity to work with them in making your life easier. So, it would be a good idea to get to know the Source of Your Being and learn to communicate meaningfully with the Presence of GOD. Letter-writing is a great way to keep in touch.

Up until now, the conversation has been one-way, in the form of the events that occur in your life, which you may not have understood. But now you can begin deepening the personal relationship with your Source in a way that is more tangible than prayer (i.e., mental thoughtforms or spoken words).

Your letters should reflect your desire to know about specific aspects of real situations in your life. All you need to do is be direct and honest. You can ask any question, the answers are available. There is no specified format for this; just write exactly what you want to say or know. Your questions should be clearly worded, and have basic direction to them. There will be no judgment, for your Source has nothing but love for you.

The purpose of the Dear Master letter is to maintain a constant awareness and dialogue with your Inner Teacher and Presence of GOD. Your teacher is responsible for providing the lessons, but *you* are responsible for taking the lessons through to their end. *You* are the only person who can create your reality.

EXAMPLES:

Dear Master,

I know that you are involved in this process of life with me. I sense that I am poised ready for new growth, and signal my readiness for some catalytic event in my life. I will be watching for your direction in revelation, dreams, direct communication or meditation, and will do my best to notice the event when it occurs. I will be constantly aware that you are with me.

Dear Master,

Thank you for making me notice the bumper sticker. I am really amazed at the synchronicity by which you bring me the answers.

Dear Master,

A dream from last night answered the question I asked. I know now that I must increase my awareness of the content of "mind chatter" and catch any limiting thoughts. Please help me.

3. Dream Log Section

The dream log is a special part of the journal because this section can give you considerable direction in your life if you use it properly. You may want to use a small tape recorder rather than directly writing the dream down. If you prefer to write it down, always have a small light and a pencil available.

Brain researchers have discovered that we dream three to ten dreams a night while in a REM state (rapid eye movement). Everyone dreams, and those who say they do not dream are not making space to receive dreams. You must declare your state of expectancy to your Subconscious Mind and Higher Self, and open your consciousness for dreaming. In our research, we have discovered that in many of our dreams, we are seeing the mind filing information.

As you become more consciously aware of dreams, your dream state will become more active. Your dreams will also become more meaningful in application. If dreams do not come easily, you may have to change your sleeping habits, or could write a letter to your Subconscious Mind about your intent.

You will notice that your dream symbology will take on the character of your daily events, for the lessons you are going through will be directly associated with your dreams. If your Middle Self is trying to block the information, it may try to cloak your dreams in deep symbology. If you want to avoid an issue in your life, you may find your dreams getting more intense and symbolic.

When you are dreaming, you are in an alpha state, so it is easy to wake up if a dream frightens you. As you pass through the hypnogogic state on waking, most dreams will fade after 30 to 60 seconds, which is why it is important to write them down or record them immediately.

As you become more aware and change your attitude about dreams, they will become easier to recall. If you do not like the dream's outcome, you can go back into the dream and rework it to change the outcome, which will actually change the future.

Here are some pointers to working with dreams:

- Before rising in the morning, make notes on the dreams you can remember. If the dream wakes you in the night, write it down. Move slowly when you are writing because you can shift from alpha to beta very fast and you may lose contact with the dream imprint. You will not lose any sleep once you get into stride. It is important to get down a sketch of every dream. The messengers will give up if you do not commit yourself to recording your dreams.
- Just get the dream down the best you can and worry about analyzing and interpreting it later.
- Write a word or two about how you felt in the dream and how you now feel about the dream. Give it an emotional value. Did you feel apprehensive, scared, confused, scolded or angry? Did it give you a feeling of joy, sadness, nobleness, or happiness? Did the dream seem to be instructive or complementary?
- Look for figures of speech, puns, or clichés. These may give the dream more meaning.
- Look for universal symbols and easily identifiable symbology.
- When you retire at night, write your question down in your dream log. This will usually invoke a dream. If the question is not answered, you may need to write a Dear Master letter about it.
- Remember you are all the people in the dream. Some aspect of you will always show up in the dream. It is possible that an important lesson could be coming to you that you would miss if you thought it was coming from someone else.

4. Inner Wisdom Section

In this section, you record your guidance and dialogue with the master teachers in your life. This may be the most pleasant section of your journal. At first you may not get many entries, but as you travel on the path, this will become one of the most important dialogue sections. This section differs from the actual Dialogue section because it is only used for recording meditation, guided imagery, revelations, or knowing that does not come from ordinary consciousness.

When you get to the point of feeling that you have your Higher Self's telephone line permanently connected to the Highest Source of Your Being (Presence of GOD), you will get direction immediately without going into meditation. You can also use this section to write a Dear Student letter from your teacher. It will be dictated to you in any form you want it to come.

This is an opportunity for you to make a close connection with your Higher Self as it is the Presence of GOD within you. When you become attuned to your Higher Self, it will give you the ability to record some of the most beautiful communication that can come as a result of perfect attunement with the GOD within. The Higher Self is the "long distance phone operator" in your universal telephone system, and will connect you to the Highest Source of Your Being. When accessing the Akashic through the Source, you can tap into any person or information in the Universe.

In this process, we are not using psychic senses, as they originate from the Subconscious Mind and the third chakra. The connection in this case is the crown chakra.

The meditation experience is in a space of pure silence. What many people call meditation is, in reality, guided imagery and when you are following a source of communication, you cannot get any inflow from the Higher Selves or your Teacher. They will not interfere in your life, and you must create a space for them to tune in, which in the beginning can only done in absolute silence, unless they have an urgent message for you, in which case, they may break in at any time. (Guided imagery, however, is useful in disconnecting you from physical reality, for you can focus on a process to step out of physical, mental, and emotional plane reality.)

Mantrum meditation is also a form to distract or move you away from your self-talk, as the focus is on a verbal attuning. Chanting is another form that will separate you from your self-talk and bring you to a place of silence. The final step in all meditation experiences is coming to a place of total silence in which all directed imagery and inner self-talk from your Middle Self and Subconscious Mind cease totally.

Meditation experiences may take many forms. If you choose to relax and release stress, it may be a quiet meditation (being careful not to go to sleep). There are two active forms of meditation: moving meditation such as dancing or movement, and writing or dialogue meditation. In the latter, keep your journal and pen handy for, if the dialogue or inspiration is in words, you will want to record it.

Not all your meditations will produce written dialogue while you are sitting in silence, but if they do, you have the opportunity to write in down. These entries may bear no connection with other journal sections, and may stem exclusively from your attunement with the Divine.

Before you meditate, you can ask any questions by writing them down in this section and taking them into meditation with you. The Higher Self as messenger will take them to the Master Teachers during your attunement and entry into meditation. The answers may be ready before you get to the place of silence.

Do not feel you must have a dialogue or a message each time. You should be able to enjoy a deeply satisfying meditation without any contact or verbal message. Do not feel disappointed if there are no words. Your teachers know when to give you the guidance you need. If you are "needy," they may withhold dialogue until you release your neediness. Put something in your meditation record each time. It may be just the quality of the meditation or the relaxation you received.

Remember the affirmation over the door of the Hall of Records: " I will bring to your remembrance all things whatsoever you have need of from the foundations of the world."

5. Stepping Stones Section (Minor Initiations)

In this section of the journal, you track your progress through life's lessons. View everything with your eyes and ears open. Then you will begin to discern how you handle yourself and the lessons before you. When you grasp that life is a workshop and that each day is your classroom no matter where you are, the lessons become easier. The Teacher provides the lessons but does not say, "This is a lesson so wake up." They are more subtle in their presentation.

The challenge is to recognize the teachers, no matter who they are—events, people, conversations, thoughts, hunches, etc. They are all orchestrated by your Master Teacher to teach you. It might not be what you would choose as your teacher, but it would not be in your life unless the lesson was before you.

An uncomfortable situation is likely to be a lesson that was presented before but you ignored it for some reason. If you are having a hard time learning the lesson or letting it go, you might want to focus more on what that particular lesson is telling you so that it is not repeated with even greater discomfort.

It is your responsibility to be aware of the lesson, and once you are, write it down in this section. Keep track of the lesson each time it comes up. If you do not recognize the lesson, scan your "Validation of Self-Worth" in the Daily Log. In a short time, you will be able to see the lessons as they come up.

This section may call for a daily entry depending on the level of your commitment to transformation. There may be days when no lesson is discernible; this is perfectly normal for you do not have to have a lesson every day. You could also slide through your life "on vacation," not recognizing *any* lessons; in fact, most people do. However, if you are not constantly on top of the lessons and recognizing them as stepping stones on the path, they are likely to get farther apart, presenting you with ever-widening gaps to jump across or ever taller hurdles.

The path is very clear and discernible when we open our eyes and ears but, just as your Master Teachers are recording your progress in your Akashic Record probably more accurately than you are doing, it behooves you to keep accurate records in your

Journal. Your Subconscious Mind is also recording everything that transpires in your life. It is automatic and you have no control over the recording process.

This is an interactive section of your journal, and it will begin to talk back to you when you find how easy it is to recognize the lessons. In fact, your self-talk might talk back to you and say, "This is a lesson; watch out and take notes." This section interacts with most of the other sections of your journal.

Look at how various lessons are presented to you. The best way to recognize the lessons is by making note of the following:

- Any uncomfortable, agitated, frustrating or emotion-packed incident contains the building blocks of a lesson. It is an opportunity to learn and take a step forward.
- If you become more acutely aware of the elements that make up your day, you will discover the lesson that you have been avoiding or putting off. In fact, the lesson may be right in your face.
- Make sure you are not projecting the lesson onto someone else or justifying it. If you do this, you're not getting it.
- If someone pushes you away or avoids you for no apparent reason, you may want to review dialogue with your self-talk and find the meta-communication that is preceding you.
- Look at how you're setting yourself up for a lesson when nobody seems to be involved. For example, you may be having fearful or angry thoughts, or running prejudice against someone or something. Review or dialogue with the thoughts or feelings that come up.
- Go back to the Discovery section and see if you can locate the incidents of the past that have invoked this lesson. If not, work with the Discovery and Dialogue sections to locate it. If it still evades you, work with a practitioner who can help you reveal the lessons.
- Write a Dear Master letter if you are unclear and you may get the answer.
- Ask for an informative dream, or ask your Source in meditation.

Teachers come in every manner of being. You could miss a pleasant friendship by preconceiving how another person will respond to you. Your conception could be false and the encounter could be a joyous happy experience with positive validation. The test is: can you handle your vulnerability effectively without fear?

In processing lessons, you will realize that you cannot make prejudgments about others until you actually meet them. Remember, you are responsible for what you say and how you react. You may say, "I create my own reality so I can say or do anything I want," and to an extent, this is true, but you are also responsible if you use people or shamelessly put them down. In the transformation process, your goal is to end separation, not create more.

There are many minor initiations (i.e., lessons) between each major initiation (i.e., turning point), and you need not master each one in order to move forward. The main lessons are about self-love, receiving love, and projecting love.

Self-validation and self-approval are most important, with the toughest lesson being accepting your own all rightness, and it will recur until this becomes a daily reality in your life. The temptations on all rightness will plague you until you decide that external validation is unnecessary. The qualities that come with all rightness are self-esteem, self-worth, self-confidence, self-validation, and self-love. These are "cluster qualities" in that they are all linked and not attainable separately. People may *appear* to have some of these qualities, but the temptation test will reveal how the person handles the lesson.

6. Discovery Section

This section documents your history from birth to present age—the raw material of your life. How did you arrive at the present place in your life? Who are the actors and actresses in your play? Have you been the scriptwriter, producer and director in your life, or have others? Who programmed your life and are you the programmer now? Can you track the cycles in your life?

The Discovery section is not a daily entry section; it is a one-time journey of self-discovery and exploration of your past, designed to map out the building blocks and the catalysts in your life experience. It also includes initiations and turning points in the past that you will also want to enter in the Turning Point section when you are able to identify them.

Few people look back at the forks in the road that they could have taken but didn't, and this is an opportunity to look back at what might have happened, but without regret. This section will take you out of the now moment into the past, for we need to understand the past and its programming before we can build a strong foundation.

Most of us are from dysfunctional families and do not have a strong foundation. Most of us hand over our personal power to Middle Self and do not deal very well with the earth plane lessons. At each fork, we took one of two paths: we either avoided the lessons of life and went into emotional/survival existence, or we skipped over all the painful earth plane lessons and jumped into the esoteric, spiritual level without dealing with the earth plane. However, a few decide to hang on and stay grounded as best they can and steer a course that will eventually guide them to the light. If you will be honest with yourself, record in this section which category you fall into, and reveal the illusions and denials in your life.

You will be adding to this section as you discover areas in your life. Take your time to build up the structure. It does not have to be done immediately. Above all, do not create more illusions and denials by building a dream of what you would *like* your childhood to have been. Many times, we put our parents on a pedestal only to have them fall when the truth begins to emerge.

Hiding in the spiritual world doesn't work either. Be as honest as possible as you can, and you may find that you have been hiding traumatic experiences from yourself. False foundations will crumble faster than you can build them. You cannot falsify your records with this system. Many times, people will block out their past because it's too traumatic. If you have a problem with going back to your history, you may need a therapist to help you.

Here are some pointers to completing the Discovery section:
1. Give a short biographical history, with a chronology of your ages.
2. Life Cycles, with the forks and crossroads. Look for the initiations, major and minor, with date, place and players. Give each cycle a title and write a brief overview. Then review your cycles now and notice if you are repeating lessons.
3. Changes within changes. Look for any series of events that brought about new awareness. Use meditation, imagery, free association or regression to locate the source of life changes and explore their lifecycles.
4. For life changes, what type of activities and relationships were happening at the time? How did you interact?
5. Initiations. (Beginning initiations are not in the 12-door process but occur when you claim your personal power.) Identify your initiations and write down how you recognized that you could be a *cause* in your life rather than a reactive result? When did you decide to step out of victim consciousness? When did you decide to handle situations in your life well? When did you decide to take charge of your life? (It could be only yesterday).
6. Turning Points, i.e., times in your life when an initiation came to fruition and you actually took control of your life. Describe the wrestling matches with whatever teacher was bringing you the lesson? Who was your angel, and your antagonist? Who was the shepherd? Who was the wise man? What gift did each bring you?
7. Review your beliefs. How many of them are copies of your parents' beliefs? Which are karmic-related? Which are your life-driving beliefs. Hint: in analyzing your beliefs, gather at least 50 to 100, involving money, sex, love, power and work. Take a good look at your beliefs about yourself and relationship to others. Separate your beliefs into two groups: those that serve you and those that do not. Then invoke the Law of Grace to discover if the latter beliefs are valid. If not, establish a new set of valid beliefs that you feel will serve you.

7. Turning Points Section

Turning Points are the major initiations in life where you demonstrate you are ready to advance through a door of initiation. In your journey on the path of transformation, you will come to forks in the road, crossroads where you know that you are taking the appropriate path in your new awareness. At these crossroads, you shift gears and begin to take control of some aspect in your life. As a child, it may have been the time you said, "I am not going to let other children bully me anymore." Or the time you decided to get good grades for *yourself* rather than to impress your parents. Of course, this spurt in your independence may not have happened until you were an adult. In fact, for many people, this does not happen until something makes them aware that they have still not claimed their personal power.

Once you decide to take responsibility for yourself and drop the need to have others validate your all rightness, you are at a crossroad and must decide who you are. Your Master Teacher will evaluate your progress, and will not accept illusions and denials.

Evaluate from the Discovery section when you arrived at crossroads or forks in your life where you decided that you would no longer put up with a behavior pattern in yourself or being victimized by others, and vowed to take control.

Turning points where you begin to relate in a different way in your life have the following characteristics:

1. You face your vulnerability and learn how to change your response-ability to emotions.
2. You claim your personal power with the ability to detach from anger, fear, etc., and respond in an effective way to an emotional situation.
3. You detach from the need to react for other people and respond in your own best interest.
4. You get to the point where you can validate yourself without the need for others' approval.
5. Your love is not dependent on another person demonstrating their love for you.

6. You can give unconditional love and forgiveness with no need for love to be returned.
7. You decide to be a human *being* instead of a human *doing*.
8. You let go of poverty consciousness, living in lack and the attachment to money. You take responsibility for your own abundance, and claim your entitlement to wealth, believing that, "God is money in action."
9. You can state the facts with no need to justify. You are all right just the way you are. There is no need to prove yourself to anybody. What is, just is.

When you complete a major initiation and pass through the door, make a note in this section with the date and the incident that you overcame that set you up to go through the door.

Make sure you have passed all the tests before you claim your victory. Many people go through a door and slip back in the testing period because they could not sustain themselves. It can be devastating to find yourself going through the same lesson when you thought you had learned it and passed the test.

Remember, *you* do not make the decision to advance through the door. As you advance through the steps, you will become aware when you are being guided towards a major initiation. You will automatically go through the door when you are ready.

You can test yourself with Kinesiology to check which doors you have gone through (see *Journey Into the Light* for requirements).

We have a Journal set up in a binder with all the instructions and page separators to begin your journal work from this chapter. (Price is $12.95 including postage. Write or call Personal Transformation Press at any of the numbers given in the order pages of this book.

16

Questions On The Process

This chapter presents questions that are frequently asked at my lectures and workshops.

Q. How can we access hidden information?

Much depends on the location of the record. For example, is it in the Subconscious Mind, your personal Akashic Record, or Collective Mind? It also depends on whether we are using muscle testing or our clairvoyant ability. With Kinesiology, you can ask a direct question. If you ask the question properly, your mind, if properly tuned, will retrieve the record you're looking for. You always get what you ask for, so your wording must be precise and specific.

I have discovered that the easiest way is to use an affirmation that directs you to the location of the information you seek. We use a specific affirmation to get to records in the Subconscious Mind or which are body-based. We use another affirmation to get to the Collective Mind. If you want to get to a future prophesy, you must recognize that the Collective Mind will only give you what is written based on past history. The future is written every day, so any prophesy reading is good for only that moment in time. The Collective Mind is based on what humanity as a whole records into it regarding the overall plan for the universe. As a collective, humanity has the free choice to change the future based on its reaction or response to it.

Q. If all this information is so freely available to us, why are so few people able to use this ability?

While growing up, most people lost the key and the instructions for their "software." Children are highly attuned to their Magical Child and the ability to plug in the phone cord to the Inner and Higher Selves, but some find it easier than others, depending on how their primary caregivers treat them. Teachers and peers often make fun of those who demonstrate a "sixth sense," which makes us abandon our intuitive ability. Having turned it off long ago, restoring it takes work and discipline, but there are specific methods we can use. The practices in this book are designed for you to retrain yourself, but many people will give up, discouraged because they feel that other people are far more gifted. However, anyone can get "on-line" to the Akashic Record.

Q. Is there a difference between psychics and those who can access the Akashic Record?

Most psychics work at the fourth-dimensional level, reading through their client's emotional field. Most Akashic readers work at the fifth dimension or higher. Another aspect is that if you want to get current updates that have not yet been entered into the Akashic Record, then develop a direct dialogue with GOD Source Consciousness through the Presence of GOD within and the Highest Source of Your Being. This will give immediate information on anybody or anything happening in that moment.

Q. If enough people hold a particular thought or belief, will that change the Collective Mind?

It has been proven over and over that if a particular thought reaches critical mass, it will change the future. Whether critical mass involves fear, negativity, and insecurity versus love, positivity, and optimism is also significant, because the latter "goes with the grain" of universal love, whereas the former goes against the grain.

Q. If past, present and future exist at the same time, how can we experience past lives?

We can read what has transpired, but it is our response that will make the difference. Every thought and action we take are recorded in the Akashic Record. We can experience a past life because the Akashic Record exists in present time so all we need do is bring up the record and re-experience it if we wish.

Some of my clients have gone into auto-regression on their own, without me needing to hypnotize them or use any regression technique. Something in their mind took them back to the time of the incident and they went through a timeline regression. Once they were in the regression, I just directed them through the experience. It could have been a past life or an earlier period in their current life.

Many describe it as if they were re-experiencing everything as it happened at the time, even down to the actual feelings. Many times, they actually act out an experience they were feeling, such as going through the death experience. I was actually able to watch them re-experience their death in complete detail.

Q. Many people have prophetic visions that are very vivid, and others literally see pictures when they do readings. If they are so real to them, why is it that the event doesn't happen?

Just because an event is entered into the Akashic Record doesn't mean it will happen, but only that is a *probability* if circumstances stay the same. Quite often, however, things change, or the people who were involved with that incident change their path. For example, a change in mass consciousness can divert the probability of an event as large as a major earthquake.

Some people have predicted earth changes for the West Coast of the U.S. supposedly starting as early as 1986 and as disastrous as the destruction of Atlantis. Obviously, that probability has not manifested, because mass consciousness shifted and did not open the door for the West Coast to break up and slide into the ocean. In many other locations in the U.S. and other parts of the world, however, earth changes are proceeding as planned. Events that cause planetary change cannot be predicted as a generalization because pockets of change in consciousness may protect that area.

Q. An event may be predicted but never happens. If everything is known, how can this happen?

Again, our mindset controls outcomes, and a change in mindset will call forth a different set of probabilities. Our responses to the events in time give dimension to it, and to make an event happen and create a record, we must participate in it, but just because an event was predicted does not mean it will come to pass. Many predictions come from reading the probabilities in the Universal Plan stored in the Collective Mind.

Humans are fascinated by the negative aspects of the future, and those who predict disasters attain notoriety, especially if they come to pass. We can change the future by the way we experience the present, and the whole purpose of being able to access the Collective Mind is to change the flow of future events that we do not want to see manifest. If enough people focus negative or positive thought forms on a future action or event, it will manifest accordingly.

Some prophets focus only on positive probabilities rather than the negative, and help bring that future into reality. I feel if enough people can focus enough attention on a single point of action in a positive manner, we can bring about positive outcomes to future events. As masters, we are responsible for changing negative outcomes. However, there are some events that will happen no matter what we do to change them, but we can moderate the harmful effects.

For example, when Jonah told the people of Nineveh that God had told him that if they would give up their fancy clothes and wear sackcloth for a specified period, God would spare Nineveh from destruction. The people listened, and the city was spared. The fall of Communism is a more contemporary example of the effectiveness of mass consciousness.

Q. Will being able to access the Akashic Record give us the ability to change our personal future?

It will not only give you an opportunity to change the future, but the way you are experiencing the present, also. Your life is acted out in as many plays as you want. The challenge is that you must take center stage and play the lead. You are also the scriptwriter, producer, choreographer, set designer, and director of all your plays. You are the only person who can affect your future. If you sell out your personal power, you are at the mercy of others. Alternatively, if enough people take their personal power and focus it on something they want to change, they can rewrite that future.

Karma is simply a lesson you set up to experience. You may have set it up before you incarnated in your current body and recorded it in your Akashic Record. If you could access that record, you could avoid the pain of the experience. GOD has bestowed us with Grace, which allows us to get the lesson and acknowledge that we understand it, but without actually going through the painful experience. Then, the Lords of Karma remove the record from the Akashic and archive it. The karma is cleared and you no longer will experience that lesson. I have found this to be more effective than guided imagery and hypnotic past life regression because we can release the lesson at the same time we are accessing it.

The way we handle our concerns about the environment demonstrates planetary karma. Earth changes are nothing more than planet Earth cleansing itself, and in 1978, I predicted that the current earth change predictions would be rendered invalid if enough people focused on and committed to changing mass consciousness. This has succeeded. A major shift in the consciousness of people has reduced the severity of predicted earth changes.

We can access the Hall of Records in many ways, but most commonly through visual imagery. But even though you may understand the lesson, that doesn't mean you can release the experience. Completing the release may need to access the body's akasha, stored in acupuncture points throughout the body. Using Neuro/Cellular Reprogramming, we can access the body's Akashic Record for the base cause, and trigger healing of most mental and physical dysfunction.

A new twist in this release process is the discovery that information is stored not only as a record, but also as encoded and encrypted messages from past lives and from parents (from the time of conception by the mother). Every feeling, thought, attitude, or conversation your mother had was recorded, and negative feelings of fear, anger or guilt resulted in encoded messages. If a mother has thoughts about abortion or doesn't want to be pregnant, this creates a series of encrypted messages. If a child feels rejected after birth or is put up for adoption, this creates an "I am not wanted" program, which sets the child up for rejection by everyone. The child will seek out those who will reject and victimize it. And as we release the self-rejection, it simply rebuilds itself. (See my book *Your Body Is Talking, Are You Listening?* for a full description.)

After much research, I have found that self-rejection can be cleared by accessing these messages in the same way that we access the records with muscle testing. Asking the right questions reveals the encoded messages, which can then be released with affirmations. The encrypted messages are connected with programs, which can be cleared using N/CR, but if the encrypted message is not accessed and released at the same time, the program and pattern will be repeatedly reinstalled.

To clear karma, we must view the record and learn how it was created. We must then declare that we understand the lesson. Once we *fully* understand the lesson, we can then claim Grace, so that the Lords of Karma can check it off in our Book of Life in the Hall of Records.

Little is written about the Akashic Record, although many cultures throughout history have been aware of it and some mystics have referred to it in their writings, for example the Book of John and the Book of Revelation.

Nostradamas (1500 AD) accessed the Collective Mind in his work, and wrote in code called "quatrains." The ancient mystery schools routinely taught this ability to their students as a way of protecting their information. In recent times, many others have demonstrated the ability to access the Collective Mind to predict the future, such as Edgar Cayce, Paul Solomon, Alice Bailey, and Ruth Montgomery.

In the last few years, Gordon-Michael Scallion and the I Am America organization and many others have prophesied about earthquakes and other earth changes. For a while, they were on track, but now, I feel that they are reading old information from the Collective Mind based on past consciousness. One person I do feel is staying up with the changes as they happen is Sean Morton. He seems to be one of the most accurate people I have met. Today, the earth plane is evolving at such a rate that future events are being constantly revised so we must have a direct line into the Source for updates.

In 1998 when I wrote *2011: The New Millennium Begins*, the records and the updates indicated that May 5, 2000 could be a traumatic turning point in the planet's evolution, but things changed. People are waking up at an ever-increasing rate, which changes the future, and as a result, May 5, 2000 turned out to be more of a personal mental/physical, emotional/psychological shift than a geological shift.

Many people are starting to feel the onset of the Quickening, which puts a tremendous pressure on people. Body frequencies have risen to over 300 Hz, which in turn stresses the endocrine system as it tries to keep you in synch with the increased speed of time. The body should operate between 12 and 18 Hz, and above that, the adrenal glands must release more adrenaline to help the body keep up. This in turn puts a major load on all systems in the body. After a while, this will cause a breakdown and possible Chronic Fatigue Syndrome or adrenal insufficiency that may lead to depression. (See Appendix C for more information.)

Another problem is that it is human nature to focus on negativity—just witness what the media focus on—and if the people contributing to critical mass are motivated by fear, then they will manifest negative outcomes. But if the critical mass is reached by people accepting they can change world events for the better, such as the World Meditation held annually on December 31, it will lead to positive, loving outcomes. We know that, together, we can rewrite future events, but the question is, what do we want for our collective future?

The need to be right is locked in the Control and Authority sub-personalities in the Middle Self. Are they willing to let go of control and see the future as being written in the present moment, with a formless state of existence?

A true mystic operates in a state of non-duality, the ability to perceive the future with no need to control the outcome, but many of us derive security from duality and control, and dropping these is threatening since we cannot lock into probabilities. So we stake our credibility on them. Based on humanity's track record, we may assume that the future will come to pass in the same manner.

In sessions with clients who have experienced many lifetimes following the same dead-end path, I often find that they have not seized the opportunity to clear lessons and lock up the records, as if they need to follow the same well-trodden path so they can predict from that experience. In other words, a known negative is better than an unknown positive. Like a broken record, they chase the same souls, lifetime after lifetime, trying to understand the lesson and clear the karma. But if they can access their records, they can understand the path and change it now. That's what Grace is all about. We do not have to re-experience the same lesson over and over in order to clear it. It is not an "eye for an eye" anymore.

The Akashic Record notes every action, reaction and response we have made in every past life, from the moment we dropped into physical reality from a spark of light. The records are like a spiritual journal, but few people read it over while still in body, so they do not learn. However, you can access your record while you are still in body, recognize your lessons, rectify the mistakes (karma), and get on with your life without suffering and pain. You are entitled to peace, happiness, joy, and harmony, with an abundance of love and financial prosperity.

The year 2011 marks the end of a 26,600-year epoch, and we must clear all the accumulated karma we have created up to this point before we can truly enter the New Millennium. Rumors abound that a new energy is going to enter our reality and sweep away all our past karma, but I have a hard time believing that our karma can be cleared without any action on our part. Humanity has gone through many epochal shifts with no history of this happening in the past. Some even believe that extraterrestrials will lift the true believers off the planet in a mass exodus and deliver them from the predicted Armageddon. Therefore, we can hold on to our anger, fear, control, justification, judgment, and attacks because some miracle is going to magically change our reality. We are going to be cleansed, so we can be perfect angels.

I feel we are being given the opportunity to correct our collective course and file a new flight plan, but we must access the records to find out what corrections to make. When a pilot files a flight plan, he checks the weather, geography, and other factors that may affect his course. If we do not monitor our course and occasionally check in with the tower (Higher Self), we may hit some big obstacles in our path. It is foolish to fly blind when a flight controller can help us avoid crashing into things.

We cannot step into the New Millennium without changing our behavior. We are responsible for our actions, and must forgive ourselves and others. We cannot brush off our past and assume that we do not have to clear the path.

At this point in time, many people want to take the psuedo-spiritual path and believe that someone will take responsibility and carry the load for them, as do fundamentalist Christians who believe that Jesus Christ died for all their past and future sins. They believe that when the Rapture and Second Coming happen, God will cause a mass exodus in which true believers will rise from their graves, along with the living faithful, and all will be carried up to Heaven. The only difference here is that extraterrestrials are not involved.

To end this chapter on a humorous note, I once saw a bumper sticker that read: THIS CAR MAY BE UNMANNED DURING THE RAPTURE. For people to think they will simply be pulled out of their cars and beamed to Heaven on some appointed date is an outrageous concept, and one that lulls people into thinking they do not have to do the work. Hindsight will tell but, unfortunately, it will be too late to make any changes when you are on the other side.

If you have any questions about the process or would like to have your questions answered in our next book, please mail or email your questions to Personal Transformation Press at the address in the Appendix.

Due to time constraints and our travel schedule, we cannot answer any questions by return mail or by phone.

PART FIVE

DIALOGUE WITH GOD SOURCE

17

Communication With GOD Source

I prefer to direct my dialogue to Source, as I feel more comfortable with that term. I went through a period of great anger towards the Christian God and felt that I was not being looked after, so I separated from the term "God."

I later came to know what GOD was, and that there was no one being to whom I could direct my questions. I also discovered that there is no supreme being that judges us so, therefore, we do not need its forgiveness. Only *I* can forgive me, and only *you* can forgive you. Once I got to the point of making my own decisions, free of belief or faith in some higher power that was judging me and wanting to control my life, I came to a new understanding of GOD.

I found that it was a loving, supportive group of beings that were not out to control my life, tell me how to run it or how I was screwing things up. They offered support, guidance, methods and tools to get out from under the load of fear, pain and anger that I carried. They always gave me lessons and opportunities to see that I could was in control and that I created everything in my life.

I was amazed to discover that we are all one and that there really is no hierarchy even though many metaphysical people have created the illusion of one. In this school we call "life," we are all teachers to each other. The more closely I identified with this Source, the more I realized that I was not separate or alone. I had created that aloneness and separation myself by rejecting the GOD Source. They had always been there for me but I had to reach out to them. When I learned how to tune in my Higher Self and get on the right frequency, life became easy.

Not everyone may agree with my description of GOD or my way of communicating with them, but it works well for the people to whom I have taught the process.

In the following dialogue, my words are in italics and the responses are in normal type.

In all my conversations with you, I notice that you refer to yourselves as "we" rather than "I." Why is this?

There is no "I," nor do we represent a single source of knowledge or information. We are a group consciousness, and are not in any way like the Christian perception of God. GOD is not a single being or entity. In fact, the definition of God that you accepted in the past does not make sense in our terms, as we are no different from you. The only difference is most of us chose not to take bodies to experience the physical world. As you have discovered, there are many perils in doing so, for most people do not have the discernment or discipline to experience your world without getting lost in the mire.

Many have gone through the trials and tribulations of the flesh in their return to our dimension to become light beings. They are your best teachers, as they have experienced what you are going through and have overcome the desires of the flesh. It is not that we are better than you; we just chose not to enter the physical world. The only difference between you and the enlightened beings that have returned to the light is that they have completed their karmic lessons and were able to become light beings again. You have that same choice.

You are able to recall that, at one time, you were one of us many millennia ago. You chose to take on a body and lost your direction. You got caught in the struggle for power and control. At this point, you have finally risen above the need for power and control so you can see the errors of your past. You are on the path to becoming a light being again. All it takes now is discipline and consistency. You have reclaimed your spirituality.

We refer to ourselves as "we" because you may be communicating with two or more of us at the same time. Also, each time you contact us, depending on your question, you may not be in contact with the same being, for some of us have more knowledge than others in certain areas, especially those who have returned from your world.

So, again who is GOD and why do we refer ourselves as plural? There is no one GOD being. We are all co-creators along with you. In fact, you have more responsibility for creating the world as it is because you participated in its downfall. We do not enjoy seeing the crime and the lack of ethical behavior taking place on your planet, but we have no control over it, nor do we want any control over it. We can only offer guidance to those who want to it and ask for it.

You are a manifestation of GOD, but you have lost those qualities that identify a GOD-like being. The qualities are still within you, but they have been overwritten with programs that block your GOD-like qualities. However, you are currently in the process of reclaiming those qualities.

There is considerable disagreement in how GOD appears to people. The Christians have their version, and various other religious groups have theirs, which causes great conflict. Why don't you manifest on Earth to reveal who GOD is once and for all, and settle all the disagreement?

How would you want us to appear?

I don't need you to manifest in any particular way. All I'm asking is for one of you to manifest in our reality and clear up the controversy.

The answer is no. GOD is everything and appears in everything. It just happens that we represent the aspect of that part of everything that communicates with you. If we appeared as an apparition, which we could do, of course, what aspect would we choose to represent the whole? Humanity would then fixate on that aspect, at the expense of all the other aspects. As we have told you many times, look around and see if you can find a person who represents what we describe as a spiritual person and you will see the manifestation of GOD. On your planet, you will have a hard time finding that person, but there are a few. Do not look among religious leaders for that person.

Could you have a person appear similar to Jesus Christ? That might solve the mystery.

As we have told you many times, there will be no Second Coming of Christ. Christ will appear among all of you and within you. We are sending many teachers to spread the word.

In the past, major teachers were endowed to teach the spiritual principles to your people, but they did not listen then, nor do they listen today. About three percent of the people on your planet have received our messages (150 – 200 million).

By flooding your planet with teachers who are on their spiritual journey, we can achieve our end goal much more effectively. Such a teacher can demonstrate to ordinary people that they, too, can do it because they see that the teacher is like them yet handles his or her life effectively. Few people would feel that they could match up to an enlightened master. However, as with all teachers, you must use your discernment.

There is considerable misconception about the term "spirituality." Many people are trying to attain that illusive quality, yet I feel there's a big difference between spirituality and the spiritual path. Would you please clarify?

Yes, there is considerable confusion between the two terms. The difference is that anyone can practice a process or follow a ritual but that does not mean that the ritual or practice is going to result in a state of spirituality. Spirituality is a state of mind that you attain by clearing all negative habits, and the need to control and have power over others. At the other end of the spectrum are codependent people who give their power away and feel victimized by others. These people are followers, for they give their power over to any guru or teacher who promises to provide spirituality for them. This, of course, is an illusion used to draw followers in. The teacher promises that if you practice this discipline or perform that ritual, you will be on the spiritual path. Yes, it may lead to the spiritual path but not to spirituality. Spirituality relies on your discipline alone, and only you can create that for yourself. Our directions are in your book *Journey into the Light*.

Understand that to achieve spirituality is a path of discipline and consistent effort to live a life without the emotional hooks that drag you down. However, the discipline we speak lies not in ritual or practice, but in recognizing the lessons placed before you and letting go of the need to be validated and accepted. The hardest lesson is accepting yourself the way you are, and then if you do not like that self, changing so that you can accept yourself.

Many people pursue distractions in their search for happiness. Should we not just be happy because we are?

Exactly. There is no reason not to be happy. That should be your natural state. You could be in peace, happiness, harmony and joy all the time if you wished. It is a choice. You do not have to *do*; all you need do is *be*, but "being" is difficult for many people. Simply being has no conditions. To explain that, you must understand that feeling happy means there is no influence drawing you down. You do not have to play any soap opera dramas to get attention. You are always able to choose the path you take. Each decision you make has a payoff unless you are at the point where you have no needs to satisfy. Unfortunately, the influences that control your decisions are always affecting the path you take. When you have no need to satisfy needs, then you can be happy because that is your natural state.

You do not need other people to make you happy. You are happy simply because you want to be. Most people operate under so much stress that happiness is alien to them, unless they live in illusion and denial, in which case, they convince themselves they are happy but lose that state when the first little crisis comes along. A happy person has no reason not to be happy. Crisis, fear, or anger do not manifest in a happy person's life. Now *that* is spirituality.

Since we are discussing happiness, how do we deal with this dilemma? Most people want to be someone, to be noticed, to be recognized for their accomplishments. Why are they not happy unless they are in the public eye?

You could answer this question yourself.

I know, but I want your opinion and some clarification.

It is the human condition to want to be recognized, so they strive to be someone, to have more than someone else, to make people admire their success. However, it is not *what you have* that counts but *who you are*. Even that can be misinterpreted if the "who you are" causes you to want notoriety. What you do must not be driven by needs or payoffs. It must be clean choice, based on your desire to do something purely because you decide to do it. We are saying that you must be free of outside motivating forces that cause you to partake in any particular situation or activity. Most people feel they are making a clean, pure choice, but often a program in the background is driving that choice. If they deny the forces driving them, or justify their choice, it will be almost impossible to discern if it is a true choice. That is as clear as we can explain it.

To be at choice, we must be free of limitations that block our options. Limitations are based in fear, and I define fear as, "False Evidence Appearing Real." Many people would say that fear is the opposite of love. In my work, I have found that the opposite of love is rejection and abandonment. Please clarify?

You found the age-old conflict. What is fear, what is love, and what is the connection? There is no connection. You have found the opposites. Lack of recognition does not cause fear. If somebody chooses to not give you love, it means that they do not want to. That could cause a feeling of rejection and abandonment in you, but does not have to cause fear if you are clear of the need for external validation.

The feeling of rejection could be momentary if you have developed self-love and recognize that nobody can actually reject you. In this case, you simply shrug it off; otherwise it could develop into a full-blown emotion, which is where fear comes into play. When you feel rejected, the fear causes physical reactions in the body, such as immune system suppression that causes your resistance to illness to drop. When the fear takes hold, it suppresses all body functions and creates out-of-control emotions. Your reactions slow down, maybe to the point of paralysis. This can result in depression.

In your society, the government, churches, and various organizations use fear as a tool to control people. That is unfortunate but you must rise above it.

Just as fear is contraction and closing, love is expansion, opening, evolving, and transforming. We will not discuss the connection between love and sex, as there is very little to say except that your culture has a complete and total misunderstanding of the relationship. There is far too much play upon sex as love, which it certainly is not. The need for love is translated into sex, which it is not. Unconditional love is given without any limitations. Conditional love has limitations, strings, and hooks. As you have found in your work, most people are unable to receive love because they lack self-love.

There are so many illusions around what love is that people sometimes will shy away from love altogether if they have limitations about intimacy. Your training as a child set the stage for your interpretation of what love is. Love is acceptance, with no need to control or manipulate, without judgment or authority. It is also kindness with caring, not the sticky, sweet syrup that has strings on it. That is conditional love. You must understand anew what love is in your culture.

The problem starts out with the biblical story of Adam and Eve. A sweet story of innocence deteriorates into judgment, original sin, and banishment, something the Roman Catholic Church has used to control you ever since. Much of the Bible destroys the concept of love so it is no wonder your society has lost its roots.

Love is a free expression of acceptance that is limitless. All healing comes through love and forgiveness. When a person truly expresses unconditional love, you can feel its vibratory quality as it breaks down all barriers that create separation. You can feel the radiation from people who express love without words.

When you step out of fear, love will encompass you. People are attracted to others who radiate that feeling of love. All you have to remember is that FEAR is "False Evidence Appearing Real." Only you can make it real. Remember it is an emotion that was taught to you. It is not in our reality. We do not use it nor do we approve its use as a tool of control. It began with religion and can stop with you!

It is your choice to make that transition to love. It may take some work. Again, this is spirituality at work.

Another big dilemma for most people is prayer. People feel their prayers are not answered. Why is it that religions always talk about prayer, yet few people get results from it?

The concept of prayer is misunderstood in your world. Most people feel that all they have to do is pray to GOD and something will magically happen. We hear your prayers, but why do you want us to do all the work? There is an element of responsibility that must accompany prayer.

Many people believe in a God that will answer their prayers. Why is that? They are hoping something will happen, yet they really don't know if it will. As you say, most prayers will not be answered. So, they are hoping that their belief will cause it to happen. It's the same as wanting. If you want something, you cannot have it. As long as you want it, you are in a state of "not having" so it cannot manifest. The answer to this dilemma is *knowing*. When you get to the state of knowing, then you can have it. Of course, you ask how can you have something that you do not have simply by knowing you do not have it? That's the catch. You have to know that you *can* have it before it will manifest. The answers are in the action. You have to go after what you desire and know that you can achieve your goal. Again it is *knowing* that causes the goal to manifest.

How about when people pray for healing of disease and illness, and most of the time it doesn't happen?

Again, it is a matter of personal responsibility. People want GOD or whatever to do something they do not want to do. Why did that person get to this condition in the first place? What was the cause?

All illness and disease have an original cause and a payoff. The root cause has to be brought to the surface. In actuality, illness and disease do not exist except in a person's mind. You have gone into great detail to explain this in your book *Your Body Is Talking, Are You Listening?*

As far as prayer is concerned, if the person actually desires healing and has no withholds to stop it from happening, it will happen. Unfortunately, most people have programs in their mind that block the healing. We have nothing to do with the healing; it happens because people choose to have it happen. We can help but they must decide that they desire to release the cause. Again, faith and belief do not *cause* healing; what does is *knowing that you are entitled to it*. You must be aware and remember we are the observers; we can provide some help, but we are not omnipotent.

This brings up the age-old question of which wins: fear or love? Most people who die of diseases are in fear. Why?

It goes back to how you were raised by your primary caregivers when you were a child. If you misbehaved yet they treated you with love and kindness, then you were accepted and validated. But if they saw you as a bad child, then fear started to enter. Fear is an emotion that is taught to you. If your mother wanted you as a child, you had no fear when you were born, but if you were rejected before you were born, you were born feeling like a reject, which precipitated into fear. You will carry this fear throughout your life unless the programs are released. Fear will win if you do not clear the childhood fear programs.

However, if you have unconditional love in your life, love will win. In the future, you will write a new book that will address this whole subject.

Many people would like to dismiss the concept that life is school or a workshop, yet most teachers I have read or studied with claim that this is reality. Is there any truth to this?

Many people would like to believe this is their only life and then they return to heaven. Others would like to believe that they have the all answers regarding the spiritual path so they need no help.

Life is indeed a workshop and every day is your classroom. Each experience has its temptations to see how you handle the choices placed before you. If you choose to avoid the lessons, you can, for no one forces you to make any soul progress. Your soul evolution is up to you. Universal Law contains spiritual principles that are guidelines but you have free choice to take any detour you want. The road to transformation can be an overgrown trail strewn with boulders or a ten-lane freeway with no traffic. It all depends on your choices.

In actuality, you are not learning anything because you already know it all. All you need do is recall what you already know. Your lives have been a devolving process where you went further from the GOD Source each time. You are now returning and learning how to go up the steps that you came down.

There are no new creations or inventions. All you need do is recall what you already know. This workshop is not an evolving process but a crash course in relearning. Your soul level of mind—the Holographic Mind—has the keys to all knowing. It is feeding back to you information as you are ready to understand it.

It is your choice to create love, harmony, happiness, and joy, or sorrow, grief, anger, and fear. They are all your creations. The workshop provides the teachers to help you remember and work things through.

You do not have to attend the seminar of life if you can figure it out by yourself. The challenge is to understand the curriculum, but few people can do so without help and coaching.

Many people go through pain that they do not have to experience. Pain is an experience that you create by how you perceive a given situation. If you could perceive it differently, there would be no pain, grief, or suffering. That may be a tough concept. It is your perception of an event or a situation that causes the outcome. You could actually be in physical pain and still be happy and joyous. The pain is telling you something. Once you understand the message of the pain, it will cease.

I'm not sure I understand. I was in pain for 24 years and I have described elsewhere how my life was in a mess. No matter what I tried, nothing seemed to work.

Did you not get out of pain when you found the teacher who showed you what created it and how to overcome it?

Yes I did, but it kept coming back unless I had treatments every two weeks. Obviously, I did not get the whole picture, even though I was studying directly under this teacher.

This was the first step in the workshop. Did you not progress further when you found the next clue to the riddle?

Yes, again. But it was not until I found the final clue that I was able to clear the pain completely. I understand that concept, but how about being in pain and being happy and joyous at the same time?

This is a good example that shows you that life is a workshop. If it had not been for the teachers who gave you the clues to each step, you would probably still be in pain and suffering. Again, perception is the key. This is also another answer to your question about spirituality. Spirituality is a state of mind, not a practice. Your state of mind is controlled by how you feel about a particular incident or experience. Martial arts practitioners can stop knives, arrows and bullets with their bare hands. Does this not demonstrate the awesome power if the mind? The mind has incredible power if you use it properly. Happiness is a state of mind. There is only pain when you perceive pain.

Yes, that's true. This can get complicated and, just because I understand what you're saying, it doesn't mean that most people will. Will you explain more clearly?

We have here what we call "shoulds" and "should nots." The first response would be, "Do not should on yourself." If pain exists, should we not feel it? It is not to say that if pain exists, you would not feel it. In our world, we see things in a different light—the light of truth. The nerve receptors in your body have been trained to experience pain under certain circumstances, but when your mind's pain receptors are cleared or blocked with acupuncture or hypnosis, the pain disappears.

In China, doctors perform major surgery without anesthesia using just the aforementioned processes. There are people on your planet working with these concepts. Again, the power of the mind and training in this workshop of life can bring forward those realities that you knew at one time.

What about limitations? Some will refuse to believe that we set our reality up. Can you explain for my readers why children are born crippled, or with Down Syndrome or Cerebral Palsy, for example?

This brings up the concept of reincarnation, which not all readers will accept. In the cases you mentioned, the soul is not creating limitations at all, but is choosing to re-experience a time in the past where it created a karmic contract or karmic agreement to handle a past life situation. Since past, present, and future exist all at the same time, the soul's path is to clear a roadblock that it created in the past and bring it up to the present so it can clear the lesson once and for all. This agreement was set up with the Lords of Karma to locate parents with the complementary lesson so that parents and child can correlate their lessons.

We have set up a process whereby you can avoid the suffering from the lesson. All you need do is understand the situation that created the lesson and ask for forgiveness, then release yourself from the lesson by forgiving and loving yourself. You may also ask for Grace to be bestowed on you and the lessons are released. If you are willing to accept that, the genetic defect can be healed and released, and your soul can get on with its journey, thereby hastening its evolution.

This goes back to question of healing. Is limitation a factor here also?

The limitation is in the inability to recognize the original cause. Your medical establishment and pharmaceutical companies have turned illness and disease into a multi-billion dollar moneymaker. What would happen if people could simply heal themselves without drugs or surgery? It would be a major blow to your economy and millions would be unemployed. Your book *Your Body Is Talking, Are you Listening?* lays out the concept well so we will not reiterate it.

You did not explain limitation very well. Could you get into that in more depth?

Limitation is an illusion created by your imagination. Do you follow that concept?

Knowing the awesome power of the mind, I do.

In the true sense of the word, limitation does not exist in our reality, for it is a concept that you take on when you accept that you are not able to accomplish something. This sets up a program in the mind that causes you to believe that you are unable to accomplish the task. This is caused purely by imagination. Remember fear is "False Evidence Appearing Real." If you buy into the false evidence, then your imagination creates a limitation program.

Imagination can be your best friend or your worst enemy. It can be a great asset to an inventor or artist, but it can be an enormous handicap because it can create programs based on its unquestioning acceptance of "false evidence" in whatever situation you are facing. It can set up programs without your approval. Unless you have taken your power back and are in control of your life, it can run wild. If you are on automatic pilot, imagination will run your life, so it behooves you take control of your life.

What about resistance? I find many people who are resisters. They either avoid situations or take action against some perceived cause or person. Buddha once said, "What you resist persists."

In dictionary terms, resistance is refusal to go along with or do something. What Buddha said was true but people do not seem to understand that if you go with something and use its energy, then you are not working against it, but defeating it by using its energy. This seems to be totally upside down according to your way of thinking, but it is so. For example, a martial arts expert will use his opponent's energy to counteract an attack. He can handle a much larger opponent because he does not resist but goes with and uses the other's energy. If you resist, you strengthen that which you resist. If you would only detach from things and situations of which you disapprove, they would cease to exist. Most people cannot accept this, so resistance will continue to be part of your life.

The opposite of resistance seems to attachment. Most people are attached to outcomes that seem to be the opposite of what you are advocating. Is that true? I know I was attached to outcome until about two years ago even though I have been on this spiritual path for over 25 years.

You must realize that you had a long tunnel to back out of, for you had dug yourself deep into the mire. We realize it has been a hard journey for you, but the key was always detachment. When you found that key nine years ago, you began working hard to let go of attachment.

Attachment is your biggest enemy. Being attached to outcome can be emotionally draining. Believing that you are engaged in right action yet being repeatedly rejected can be traumatic. Today, however, you can stand up for yourself but be detached from the outcome. You know that the best will come from every action and that the appropriate result will manifest, but that you are not responsible for that result. Have you noticed that?

Yes, especially with my books. In the last year it has changed. Now that I have let go of trying to push the books, we are getting some huge orders. It's happening at all levels of my life, too. It's great to no longer worry about whether I will have enough money to make the house payment and pay my other bills. What I want to understand is, why was it when I was not on a spiritual journey that I had no troubles with money and many other aspects? Life was easy until I embarked on this journey to find myself. Then, it seemed as if everything that could go wrong did. We lost 30 years of life-savings, our home and our business. In a few short years, we were reduced to survival level. We gave our life over to service but life seemed to beat us up and reject us. The last 12 years have been particularly tough.

That "ignorance is bliss" is very real. The only problem with this is that you make no soul progress in your life. When you do not open yourself up to the lessons of life, little growth comes your way. Be realistic. Were you really happy and satisfied with life as it was?

On the surface, we seemed so happy and everything seemed come to us as if it was supposed to be that way. Money was easy and life was rather enjoyable. But, underneath, it was an emotionally traumatic time because we were living in a lot of underlying stress. I had no idea what love was, so we were in a codependent relationship. On an inner level, this was uncomfortable. But we were in denial, so it did not exist. I can see what you mean now. Please continue.

You now see the benefit in what has happened. If you review the past, you can see that most people live on autopilot. Some people do get what they want, but they are attached to outcomes. The happiness you found is not money-oriented even though it may seem that way.

When you decide that it's time to clear out the closet, all the issues come tumbling down, issues not only from this life, but from countless other lifetimes of denial. When you started on your journey, two of your teachers remarked that you had selected a trajectory like that of a space rocket. Was that true?

Yes. Everything seemed to come up all at once, but I was not willing to give up or stop. We kept on going, taking the risk to step onto the spiritual path by opening a metaphysical bookstore and counseling center.

It was a flamboyant step to take and you may have been overstepping your bounds at that time because what happened was predictable. You were too attached to the outcome. This was the message when it seemed as if the world was trying to stop you. However, you refused to get the message even when you lost your house the first time. You were getting all your validation from running the center. You did not see this fact so when it was in danger, you went even deeper into debt to try to rescue it. It had to be actually taken away from you so you could see the level of your attachment, but even then, learning that lesson took you another eight years. When you embark on the spiritual journey, you signal "I am ready," and the lessons will come up. The fear of that keeps many people from starting the journey.

You frequently use the words" journey" and "spiritual path." Would you please explain the connection or difference in the terminology?

"Journey" refers to the process of the experience you are traveling on in your soul's evolution. "Spiritual path" refers to a specific practice that you undertake to learn by. "Spirituality" is the result of learning the lessons that are presented to you and letting go of the emotional attachments that have held you back. Spirituality is the substance of your life when you reclaim your personal power and the cluster qualities as you have described them: Self-Esteem, Self-Worth, and Self-Confidence. This will give you the confidence to let go of control, judgment, justification, manipulation, justification, blamer, need for power, being a victim and all thirty of the other emotional crutches that run your life.

When you arrive at the point where you can validate yourself and you have no need for others to like or accept you, you are reclaiming your spirituality. Unconditional love becomes the way you treat yourself. When other people see this quality evident in you, they will do the same for you.

It is an inside job. No teacher, guru or shaman can give it to you. No spiritual practice can provide this to you. In fact, you do not need to be in a spiritual group to obtain this quality. When you get there, it is quite evident, as you will have no need to be accepted or be anything. When you no longer transmit the need to be accepted, people will respond. This is not something that someone can teach you or give you. You have always had your spirituality, but you had to reclaim it by deleting, erasing and destroying the programs that you had written over it, which rendered it temporarily unavailable to you. Have you noticed that ince you did this, those qualities came into your life?
Yes, it began to happen last year. It's amazing how easy it is to say

what you want to say and have no attachment to a desired outcome. In the past, I would have strived for acceptance and approval. I was appreciative of what I received, but it was hard to accomplish. Now I can say that if what I want doesn't come about or manifest, I have no sense of loss, rejection, or abandonment as I did in the past. Of course, I would like people to accept me and support me, but it now makes no difference whether they do or they don't. It seems as if when one door closes, two more open, sometimes with even more opportunities or better situations.

Do you understand attachment now? It is an elusive quality to most people because they have needs that they want met. Whether or not you know what those needs are makes no difference. If they are beyond your recognition or in denial, you won't even know they exist. If the needs are active programs in your mind, they will cause situations to manifest even though you are not aware of why they come up.

The behavior may not be what you would have chosen, but it will continue to come up until you locate the sub-personalities and the programs that are driving them and clear them.

If readers were looking for a teacher who could impart this knowledge, what or who would they be looking for?

This is an interesting question as teachers are often not who you think they would be. Let us describe who you would *not* be looking for first. Their level of notoriety or stature is irrelevant, as is the number of books they may have written. Their apparent level of spirituality is also irrelevant if they cannot present their knowledge properly.

What would you look for, then? True master teachers are those who can duplicate themselves and impart their knowledge to their students with no fear of the students equaling or surpassing them. The test is then is not how many students they have, but how many of those students evolve into master teachers themselves. Rather than counting how many followers they have, look how many people have they empowered to become leaders.

Evaluate their life path to see if they have their own lives together and walk their own talk. There are exceptions to this rule, such as when master teachers do not walk their talk because they separate their personal life from their teaching position. They can still impart their knowledge without allowing their personal life to affect their teaching, but this take a heavy toll on them and will usually result in an early death due to the stress placed on the Mind/Body.

You know who we are talking about, don't you?

Yes, two of them, and they changed our direction for both of us. In fact, when I came home from the first seminar, my behavior had changed so much that my wife asked me if she could attend the next seminar.

Teachers like Paul Solomon and Ronald Beesley are rare. You were blessed to be on the journey when they were alive. Not many people find teachers of the caliber of these two. Most teachers are satisfied with what they have learned and do not continue to be open to new concepts, as did those two.

You mentioned earlier that we would not always contact the same GOD being each time because different beings would be consulted regarding specific areas. What do you have to say about that?

That is true. You could be one of these beings, too, as these beings have all gone through "the tribulation" as the Christians call it. They have become light beings and risen to the spark of GOD so they are in a level of enlightenment. As a result, they are one with the GOD Source. There's no discrimination in our reality. Beings that can go through the lessons and activate the Presence of God within can achieve the transformation that will move them through the transfiguration so that they become part of the GOD Source.

This is an amazing destiny to strive for, and to know that it's available to everyone is even more wonderful. How do we get on this track to the lofty levels you have described?

Why are you asking this question when you know the answer?

I felt it would add credence if you answered the question.

Well, we are not going to answer the question because it will take too much space and, with our support, you have already written a book on the subject. So we refer you to your book *Journey Into The Light*, which provides the information we have given you.

I was asking this question for benefit of the readers of this book, but I can see the reasons for your answer.

This would have been a lengthy answer since entering the spiritual journey encompasses many concepts.

I have been disappointed in people who make commitments and never follow through. What do you have to say about right relationship and intent?

This is one the biggest challenges in life. Some people do take their commitments seriously, and understand ethics and integrity, but it seems that many people see nothing wrong in not following through with their commitments. The issue here is relationship with self; basically, they have none. Your relationship with self is the most important relationship you have.

Life proceeds out of your intentions, and if you have no goal, no direction and do not know how you are going to get there, you have no relationship with self. These people feel like victims, that their lives have no direction. This is because your life is a result of your thoughts, feelings, actions, and intentions. When most people encounter a person whose life is working, they feel resentment. They look at his life and see him getting what he wants out of life, so they see themselves being denied the joys and abundance in life. They fail to see that the difference is a matter of attitude, so they say, "You should provide for me because you have it and I don't."

This attitude is the basic cause of deterioration of your society. Most people do not have a right relationship with self and they feel victimized by those who *do*. Those who feel that others are more fortunate are lost in their victimhood. Your religions and government are notorious for fostering this attitude. Welfare has created a society of have-nots who feel that society owes them a living. Organized religion tells you that you were born in sin but gives you a savior who died for your sins, so you do not have to take personal responsibility for your actions.

Why should people make commitments and follow through when society tells them that it's okay to blow off commitments. Their Justifier sub-personality justifies all their behavior and then denies any wrongdoing, so their mind pigeonholes the program in the denial-of-denial area of the mind and the commitment is erased. The victim mentality behind of all this is rooted in anger and resentment, but the person does not understand or recognize this.

The only way out of this is to recognize the behavior, and then release the anger and resentment. It may even involve anger at what they perceive as God. These people must first recognize the lack of relationship with self, and then seek help in releasing the cause. Does that explanation help?

Yes, thank you. It seems that many people cannot see their way out of this dilemma because they can't even recognize the problem. How can you ask for help when you don't even know you have a problem?

When you do not recognize the problem, you cannot. It is a sorry state that your society has fallen into, but you must not let yourself get caught in the problem. Help those you can, but do not let yourself be drawn into resentment or being victimized.

Remember that you created it all. You decided to make a commitment with a particular person simply because you wanted to or there was a desired payoff. Remember that you create all situations in your life.

Robert Ringer's book, Looking Out For Number One, *offered more common sense advice than spiritual guidance, but in the spiritual field, we would call his approach self-centered rather than caring. What is your feeling?*

To be self-centered is the ultimate level of focusing on soul evolution. People are either outer-directed or inner-directed. Inner-directed people do not need anything from others, for they are self-validating and are usually able to love themselves. They are more self-centered, in that they are centered in self. They ask nothing of others, as they are able to take care of themselves. They do not care what others are doing, wanting, or owning. They ask very little of other people as they can recognize their own value and have right relationship with self. They are often more loving because they have no need to take, and thus have more to give. Their relationships seldom fail because they have no need to draw from their partner.

On the other hand, outer-directed people are "other-centered" because they need everyone to support them for they do not love themselves and constantly look for others to validate them and offer approval. They actually dislike themselves because they feel unloved, for they must work at drawing love out of others. Even when you give them love, their self-image may be so poor that they cannot accept it. In fact, some will even believe that the only reason you are giving them love is because you want something. They get lost in relationships because they have no clear self-concept and let the relationship define who they are. This is actually a sickness when it turns into addiction, for they then see their partner as the "medicine that makes their life work."

In order for a relationship to work, both partners must see themselves as worthy. When you become self-centered, then you have right relationship with self. Of course, society seems to have this backwards, and heaps guilt on to those who are self-centered, but this is due to ignorance. One who was truly self-centered would not participate in man's inhumanity to man, such as slavery or the crimes and cover-ups committed by government officials and business leaders.

Truly self-centered people honor the self, are in right relationship with self and behave with integrity and honesty. All we see among your supposed leaders is greed for power and control, and an attitude of, "I'm going to grab what I can while I can."

The self-centered behavior we advocate involves honoring self rather than controlling others.

Religionists argue that God created us as imperfect beings and then sent his son to Earth to "fix his mistake." Does that make any sense?

Absolutely none at all. This could be a long answer, but we will try to keep it short. First, let's set the record straight. Most emphatically, we did not send the person you know as Jesus Christ to correct a mistake we made when we originally created you.

We have written many books with the author of this book that explain how the whole process of life began, so we are not going to reiterate that. What we want to make clear here is that a historical person called Jesus Christ did not exist by that name. That was a creation of the Roman Catholic Church. The teacher on which the story is based was similar to many of the other wandering teachers whom we have sent to you in order to get our message across about love and forgiveness. We have tried with many races and in many languages in the hope that the message would be spread throughout your planet. Judging by how people treated these teachers and their wisdom, we have obviously failed. How many government and church leaders have a right relationship with self? Very few.

Of course, the man they crucified 2,000 years ago was an enlightened master teacher so he could control what happened, yet he allowed himself to be tortured and killed. Isn't that a dichotomy? When he said, "Do not judge them as they do not know what they are doing," he was clearly saying to the world that no matter what they were doing, we should forgive them as he did. He set the whole crucifixion scenario up to demonstrate a concept that he was trying to teach the people. Did they get it? No. So he came back to show them that he had not died. They were so blown away by his demonstration that they described it as a miracle. In fact, he did not die in the first place but was nursed back to health by his Essene brethren.

So what's the message? Simply that you need leaders who are in right relationship with self so that you can rise out of the mire in which you are trapped. A few leaders give us a glimmer of hope, but most of your people do not seem to hear them too well. If you do not get the message soon that you must operate from ethics, integrity and honesty, you may destroy your species and even the planet, as you have many times in the past. However, we see another scenario emerging as your planet begins to evolve to the next dimension. It is a race to see which happens first: ascension or destruction.

Wow. You really wound up in that response.

This is a sore subject for us because we have tried every angle we can to get the message to your people. You have the teachings and the knowledge to bring your planet and its people out of their downward spiral yet you're doing a poor job of getting it started. We do have faith, however, that some of your people are getting a glimmer of the message but unfortunately they are not in positions of control, although we do see some leaders emerging soon.

Since you were so agitated about this last dialogue, I have another related question. I have been communicating with you for over 20 years. At this point, I know I should accept that what you tell us is true since it has proven itself over time, yet there are times when I doubt what I am receiving. It sometimes seems to me that I'm making up our dialogues, even though experience proves that I am not. Can you assuage my doubts?

Firstly, you cannot prove that we exist nor can you prove that what we tell is the truth until it has proven itself over time. Even time is irrelevant because it only exists in your dimension so that you can anchor an experience or a situation. We, however, operate in timelessness.

We know this is redundant, but has anybody ever been able to prove there is a GOD? Many things that exist in your universe are not provable at this time. You have already experienced a situation with your invention of the Harmonizer. We helped you to invent a unit that defies physical science, yet science must admit that it does what we said it would do. You cannot see how it interacts with the physical body and the neurological system, yet it causes changes in the endocrine and immune systems, and stabilizes blood pressure. It has myriad effects on the physical body yet there is no observable agent that you can see, unlike the pills you take.

Do you really need physical evidence of who we are? We could create many forms of aberrations for you to see, but what would that prove? Nothing. In fact, if we did, many people would call it the work of the devil or Satan.

You seem to accept at this point that the traditional God of the religionists does not exist. We have clearly explained who we are and what we represent. Is there anything else we need to say? Do you have any suggestions as to how we could prove to you who we are?

I have come to the point where I accept what you say and do not need proof. I feel that what has happened in my life journey over the last twenty years is enough proof. I have very seldom felt the need to see a therapist because your group is the best therapy I know. Of course, that's if I can get into the calm space needed to listen and respond to the advice and direction. All in all, I am confident in my connection, which is why I decided to write this book. I want people to understand that I am not special, nor do I have special gifts. Anybody can do what I do.

It is interesting that you put it in those terms, for many of the people we talk with want names and handles to identify us by. You are one of the few people who are satisfied with the fact that we are able to give you what you want with no fanfare. We can see that your spiritual journey has been tough at times, but now that you have gone through the worst times, it will be much easier.

Knowing who we are on this path is a real tough lesson. Most people seek outside validation because they don't know who they are. I am over the hump in knowing who I am, but still get into conflict with people who accuse me of acting in a know-it-all manner. Since I don't want to come off like this, how do I handle the situation?

The basic problem is that others perceive you as a threat. You trigger inner conflict in them since their inner self knows you're right but their conscious mind doesn't want to accept your self-validation because, to their way of thinking, it diminishes them in their eyes. Most people are constantly comparing themselves with others and, in their eyes, they frequently take second place in the competition. They then reject themselves as "losers" and blame you for how bad that makes them feel. They felt fine until you showed up, so it must be your fault.

This goes back to your question about outer- and inner-directed people. When one of each type interacts, the outer fawns over the inner, trying to elicit approval and acceptance. When the inner does not give that approval, and does not seek approval from the outer, the outer interprets this as the inner saying, "You do not matter to me. You are not interested in my opinion or input."

Of course, this interpretation is 180 degrees wrong, because inner-directed people most certainly *do* pay attention to other people, but not in a way that outer-directed people recognize. For example, during a conversation, most people do not listen to the other person but are thinking of what they're going to say when their turn comes so that they can look good and steer the other person into giving them some validation. If they can dominate the conversation, they are being validated because everyone else is listening to them.

You do not have a choice as to how others accept you. Your only choice is how to respond. If they react negatively to you, your only response can be, "That is your interpretation and you have the right to your opinion. Whether or not you accept me or my concepts makes no difference to me. I do not need your approval."

Of course, to people who do not have a right relationship with self, you will appear smug and self-righteous, and your not needing them to validate you will bring up feelings of inadequacy in them. There's no way round this, so console yourself with the thought that, to other inner-directed people, you sparkle with happiness and joy. You can't have it both ways.

There is another question that really pushed my reality a few years ago. When Wayne Dyer published his book, You Will See It When You Believe It, *his thesis was that you must first believe something before you can experience it. That seems to be true since people will deny facts even though they are clearly evident.*

It may not be evident to those who deny facts that are clearly in front of them but it happens so often that it's amazing. This again, is caused by fear. Accepting all the facts or situations presented to them would completely destroy the tenuous belief systems to which most people cling. Many people have such a fragile belief system that they must exclude clear evidence in order to function in life. Crop circles, for example, are an obvious fact, yet their existence raises so many unanswerable questions that many people ignore them in order to cling to their sanity. Many find anomalies like that threatening.

Similarly, if people choose not to accept something because they cannot allow themselves to accept or understand the situation, they truly may not see it. This is a reversal of the old saying: "I'll believe it when I see it."

In order to accept something, you must be able to place it in some familiar pigeonhole in your belief system. If you cannot do this with crop circles, for example, your only alternative is to deny that it exists, and then for you, it truly does not exist.

Returning to the question of the existence of a God, many believe in it even though they cannot prove it or see it. It's a matter of getting to the point where "you know that you know." A great sage once said, "All knowing is from experience," but this not quite accurate. You can only experience who we are by communicating with us, because we do not manifest in your life. Therefore you can only know us by acceptance. So this is a valid paradox. Once you have seen who we are, you can believe who we are.

Many people believe in a God but cannot accept that they can talk with it. They do not have the knowingness since they are operating from belief. When you tell them that *they* are the Presence of GOD, how do they react?

Most people cannot accept that they could be at that level of consciousness. You cannot be at the same level as something you worship. Some even accuse me of blasphemy. Knowingness and beingness are tough points to get across to a person who has strong beliefs about a subject.

That is why your society has broken down the way it has. People operate from false beliefs and illusionary concepts. They have lost their sense of self so they grasp for something that can give them comfort and the illusion of joy and happiness. In your society, that means money and sex. In the mad scramble to find something that makes sense, people have lost the concepts of ethics, integrity and honesty. They are now just old-fashioned ideals.

Thirteen years ago, when you were down and out with all the lessons hitting you at once, you were provided for. Did you feel fear and despair at the time?

Plunging from abundance to poverty in three years was a unique experience. It was as if we had no control over the events in our lives. There was some fear but we did not give up nor did we ask for any assistance. However, many people came to our aid and we pulled out. During our return to awareness, the lessons were heavy and difficult but the breaks seemed to come at the oddest times. We just took each day at a time. As a family, we operated as a unit and had the knowing that we would see our way clear in the future. The lessons were costly and turbulent at times, but we did not give up. We went forward each day knowing we had support. Some days, though, we did feel abandoned, but we always kept our eyes on the horizon and knew that "this too shall pass."

This is a good example of the "dark night of the soul" that everyone on the spiritual journey must go through. The degree of discomfort depends on how many lessons you avoided in the past. You will draw the lessons to you when you least expect them. They never go away, but just wait until you're ready to handle them. You have only so many "time-outs" in a lifetime, however, and you had used all yours up, so everything hit you at once like an avalanche. Many people go through many lifetimes before they wake up to the fact that they have to deal with old unfinished business.

So, what you're saying is that I created the avalanche by putting off the lessons in the past, but I don't recall doing that.

As you know, your multi-faceted mind can go off many directions until you have unification in your mind. When you reclaimed your personal power and took control of your life, your mind was still not aligned, even though you were aware of what alignment was. As a result, you still did not have full control of your life. Because you didn't know about the necessity of facing life's lessons, you avoided them and they stacked up. You didn't know that by avoiding the lessons, you were using up your time-outs until you ran out. Your Higher Self and Holographic Mind knew about the lessons but you were not listening to them. You were operating out of your Survival Self, which most people do, but Survival Self always makes its decisions on the emotional level. Also, it assumes that it can handle your life better than you can, because you gave your power to it when you were a child.

When you decided that you did not want to be in physical pain any longer, you started looking for a way out. Conventional medicine brought no relief, so you decided you were ready to locate your flight plan. At this point, your Conscious Mind decided that there must be a way out, so you began to look for it. But, as in the old adage, "When the student is ready, the teacher appears." That is exactly what happened and the rest is history.

My opinion is all emotions are negative experiences. We can learn from them but they do not support us in any way. They all have a payoff or achieve some objective. What is your opinion?

All emotions come from one source—fear. There are 25 subgroups of fear as you have described in your books, and all are

tied into loss of something. That's why using the emotion offers a payoff or something to gain. For example:
- Anger is a reaction to loss of control and an attempt to regain it.
- Grief is a reaction to the perceived loss of something. In fact, you do not lose anything, but your piece of mind is upset by the loss, so you go into grief. When you let go of the loss, it disappears. People can wallow in their loss for years, not seeing that they are creating the emotion. No one is doing it to you. You are in total control of the whole situation.
- Envy is a reaction to something that someone else has that you also want.
- Jealousy is also a reaction to something that someone else has, but in this case, rather than wanting it too, you do not want the other person to have it so, in the extreme, you try to take it away from them.

All emotions are reactions to wanting something you do not have or regaining something you have lost. However, this does not apply in the case of love. Love is not an emotion even though many people call it that. Love is not a reaction, but a pure force of the universe.

With love, you have not lost anything nor does desiring it help you obtain it. Love has no emotion to it because love's very definition makes it inaccessible to people who are running emotion. *Love is kindness and caring, with no need to judge, control, or manipulate.*

Love is acceptance without any need for "authority over" the beloved. If there is a need to satisfy some emotion, then it is conditional. Forms of conditional acceptance could be misinterpreted as love as they have emotions attached to them. Love has no need to change the beloved or their behavior. It is total unconditional acceptance with no strings or hooks attached.

Are emotions taught or are they natural reactions?

If a baby was accepted and wanted before it was born, then after it is born, it has no emotional responses. At birth, if it bonds with the mother, this confirms to the baby that it is wanted and loved. It has no fear or anger.

The responses that the primary caregivers provide determine the responses that are created by the baby's mind. If the baby has developed trust from the love and bonding that were accepted from the mother, then no negative emotions will be exhibited. A baby will assume that it can trust the mother until she proves otherwise. As long as she responds to the baby's need for love and acceptance, it will not create emotional reactions. If she expresses any anger or fear, the baby will react to that stimulus and begin to accept emotions.

As we said before, emotions all stem from fear. They are created when a stimulus causes them to react. As people take control of their life and reclaim their personal power, they are able to release themselves from emotional reactions. At times, fear does serve a purpose in that it stops you from doing something that could threaten your life. Getting mad about something can provide the impulse to change something, but if it persists for any length of time, it can degenerate into an emotion fueled by the feeling of loss.

All emotions are attempts to gain something that you have either lost or do not have. There are no positive emotions. But, as we have already said, you cannot have something and want it at the same time. You either have it or you do not have it.

There is basic disagreement in this area, for few people have the ability to love themselves or receive love, so they react by turning love into an emotion. In this way, they can experience what they think is love. Passion is passion; it is not love. Sex is sex; it is not love. Passion and sex can lead to love as long as people know that they do not create love.

Relationship and sex addiction stem from people not feeling fulfilled in their relationship with self. When people do not have right relationship with self, they begin to look for another person to provide the missing link, to satisfy the need. If people do not recognize that the need can be filled only temporarily with conditional acceptance, they will keep looking unsuccessfully for someone to fill the need that, of course, never gets filled. This is commonly known as codependency, one of the greatest and most frustrating addictions because the need for validation and love are never filled.

With relationship addiction, one of the most damaging and destructive emotional traumas occurs where the partner becomes the medicine. People can actually become psychotic in their belief that the person of their desires is the only one who can fill this need. This can lead to feelings of ownership and control, and if they get rebuffed or rejected, some people react so violently that they have been known to kill the person that they cannot have. This is epitomized in the words, "If I can't have you, then no one can."

In sex addiction, many people feel the only time they are loved is during sexual union. This is delusion for, as we've seen, sex is not love. Your society has created a total misnomer in the phrase, *"making love."* You cannot "make" love; it exists in of itself. Love is an energy, not a physical action. It is a quality that one expresses through caring and kindness, not manipulation and control.

Does that answer the question?

Yes, thank you. My experience has been that few people have love working in their life so they give up the desire and shift their need to food, control, and manipulation.

Have you noticed that most people in the West are overweight?

Yes, that's an obvious commentary on the lack of personal responsibility and running on autopilot. What can one do about this dysfunction?

The work you have been doing is one way to treat this need. People must get in touch with why they are compulsive over food, because dealing with obsessive behavior is difficult when you do not understand the cause. The primary cause is lack of love, so a person uses food to satisfy the need to feel good. If you notice what overweight people eat, you will understand why they are obese. Another reason for excess weight is that the body loses its ability to digest food properly so the digestive system absorbs simple sugars rather than the wholesome nutrients. As a result, even if they eat a good diet, they may continue to be overweight. It's all contained in the programming.

People seem to be confused about physical desires, the mind's logical choices and what the Higher Self would choose for us if we were aware of the best possible path to take. What are the implications?

Few people know what's best for them, which is why your planet is in such chaos. Physical desire drives most people, and since they are on autopilot, they will choose that which provides the most pleasure. If Middle Self drives the programs all the time, then you see even more body-centered activity.

Logic does not come from higher mind; it is a learned activity. Logic is a response pattern where a person learns to think in a certain way. Because the pattern is learned, you would assume that higher mind is driving it, yet you can teach a monkey to be logical but it's not coming from higher mind. Logical thinking is inner-directed and does not always result in ethical or appropriate action unless the person has a developed a belief system that leads to ethical action.

If people were coming from Higher Self, then they would do everything in integrity with concern for the well-being of others. If they were to make the appropriate choices in alignment with soul evolution, they would let go of limitations and attachments. Inner-centered thought is independent of how other people accept or validate you. Outer-centered behavior, however, comes from a lower level, as it requires approval and validation of others.

Receiving guidance to take appropriate action can also be an illusion, as there are many voices out there that are not coming from our level of consciousness. If you are to depend on Higher Self to direct your life, you must first correctly connect to it. Many people wrongly assume that Higher Self is directing them to us.

There are many entities out there that do not have your best interest in mind. They gladly offer you advice, yet is it accurate? The entities will tell you that they are acting your best interest, but can you trust them? Coming from higher mind requires that you do daily exercises to keep yourself tuned to your Higher Self.

There is considerable debate today about raising children in our mobile society. The argument concerns the love of the nuclear family unit being eroded by career-oriented relocation, so now, extended families end up spread all over the country. Some people feel that family elders such as grandparents should raise children because they have more wisdom and time. What's your take on the issue?

Yes, this is a very controversial subject. Since you live in the United States, you have witnessed the breakdown in the family unit over the last fifty years, but this is not the case around the world.

First, look at how a child responds to bonding with the mother. Realize that a child's early life is controlled by the mother's thoughts, feelings and actions during pregnancy. Her relationships with everyone around her, and their feelings toward the unborn child will create prenatal programs in cellular memory.

Bonding with the mother at birth is very important to the child's development, and in less "developed" cultures, the mother spends the first four years literally carrying the baby everywhere. A harmonious relationship with caring parents greatly impacts the child's future. And in tribal cultures, the birth of a child is marked by celebration and ritual, all for valid reasons today forgotten in the so-called "advanced" industrialized countries.

In today's Western world of two-career households and focus on women's rights, fewer women are having children at young ages. And in a career-oriented culture, children receive short shrift. Some women want to have children and a career, too, but it doesn't work. The mother should be with the child for the first five years of life, three years at the very least. The father can substitute, but it doesn't have the same effect. Bonding with the mother has a major effect on a child's later life.

After age five, it's less important as the child is beginning to break away and create a relationship with self. If women want a career, they should, but not mix it with having children at the same time. Get established in your career, take a sabbatical so the children can have quality time with one or other of the parents, and then return to work.

Children who do not have one or both parents to provide good models for them will suffer from low self-esteem, self-worth, and self-confidence, leading to a feeling of "I'm not all right," to, "I don't fit in. They don't want me," all the way to, "I am a reject. I have no value."

If children have a good foundation built prior to starting school, having a parent there for support is not as important once they start school. At age five, they begin to build a sense of self, and prior training determines whether they build strong self-esteem or become victims. We can't emphasize enough the importance of the first five years. They mold the rest of children's lives and control their direction as adults.

We will not discuss the detrimental effects of poor parenting or abusive parents for enough has already been written on that subject. We just want to get across the importance of having the mother with the children for the first five years.

You make the point well. With our children, we took turns parenting and being with them during their formative years. It proved out as you say. Today, as young adults, they have self-esteem and self-worth beyond our expectations.
Some people insist that parents who are children themselves and are not equipped to raise children cause the breakdown in the family. The elders who have the experience and the wisdom to handle the task should raise children. Parents should get into their careers and leave raising the children to the elders, who have the ability to handle them. What's your perspective?

We just said that the breakdown of your society stems from the splitting up of the larger family grouping. In the days past, people rarely moved from their town or village, so the extended family lived together or in close proximity to the family elders. The elders helped raise the children but they were not the primary caregivers.

During WWII, this all began to change as women started working in offices and factories. In the postwar shakeup, many of them chose to continue working, but mistakenly tried to mix this with being a mother.

Many people will disagree with us, but please realize that we're not just talking about recent history. We have been observing problems that have developed over many thousands of years. As we said before, the breakdown of the nuclear family is unique to a few industrialized countries, and most societies on your planet still operate in the traditional manner.

We see no difficulty in a mother having a career before she has children or after they are grown. Nursery and pre-schools can provide good socialization training for children but there is no substitute for mothers who can give children the love, acceptance, and validation they crave.

Most childhood illness is caused by the unmet need for attention. Once the program is established in the child, it will continue until it is erased and deleted. Most illness and disease stem from childhood feelings of rejection and abandonment.

Children will not respond to other caregivers in the same way that they do their mothers. It was evident in the period between the 1930s and 1950s when children were placed in orphanages. Some died for no apparent cause, but the real reason was rejection by the mother and lack of love. The soul decided that there was no reason to stick around so it left. This is also the reason for stillborns and when children die early, even when they are with their parents. Children must have love and acceptance, and if they don't, problems arise.

Returning to the original question, elders are sometimes no better equipped to raise children than the biological parents. If they were from a dysfunctional family, then their children will be raised in the same manner. There are exceptions, of course, but few people really know how to raise children. Why do you think family and society have broken down? It is not solely because parents do not know how to raise children. It is the history of your planet repeating itself over and over.

The degradation of the family unit has been going on for many thousands of years, and is nothing new. However, increasing greed for power and control have accelerated it. It is tied in with how your religions and political institutions oppress women. They are finally rebelling and claiming their power, but this has a major effect on the children.

Again there are always exceptions, but it is more prevalent in the West. The less civilized societies still enjoy more cohesiveness in the family unit and, in fact, "less civilized" is a western judgment that places people in the western world at a higher level.

We have observed that civilizations fall when the family unit is destroyed. You can see it in your own country over the last fifty years. Also, let us point out that, as the family unit deteriorates, the elders have no place and may feel that they are a burden on their children.

I have seen it happen in my own family, so we decided to stop the vicious cycle. We are only the first generation in this new pattern, but at least we reversed the deterioration. We did not realize what we were doing at the time, but simply decided that our children would not be raised the way we were. I feel that parents should get settled before they have children, so we delayed having children until we were in our mid-thirties. We became financially comfortable and did some traveling to find out where we wanted to settle before we had children. What's your opinion on this?

You took a wise path. You got your traveling out of your system before you had children so that you did not feel tied down. It is important that two people get to know each other before they settle down. It's hard to raise children when you're trying to make it financially and grow up yourself. Most people still behave as children until they're in their thirties. In fact, some *never* grow up, as in the term coined twenty years ago, "adult children." These people should not have children until they grow up themselves. If they do not seek help and get their life settled, maybe they should never have children. Let us say that you would have a much better adjusted society if people would get their feet on the ground having children. If this means waiting until age 35, so be it.

Your patriarchal religions contribute to the problem, too, by advocating keeping women in the home. This has an underlying flavor of control since the men do not want to be threatened by women reclaiming their personal power. In fact, many men do not want to participate in taking care of children and claim, "That's the woman's job. I don't do that."

Raising children is a 50-50 proposition because they need attention and love from both parents. They also need the elders' love and attention, too.

Does that clear up the questions?

Yes, it does very well. I have another question on the same subject. The beliefs of some religions result in large families, and this overextends the parents' financial capability. Ideally, how many children should comprise a family unit?

Many religions' views on abortion and contraception lead to large families, and the planet's population is growing too fast, especially in poorer countries that cannot afford to care for their citizens. The ideal family would be two children, so as to replace the parents without increasing the population. Ideally, children should be five years apart so that a child has time to develop a relationship with self before a sibling comes along. Children born closer together than this often feel rejected and abandoned at the birth of a new sibling.

Many will disagree with this, but with some exceptions, our observation is that self-esteem and self-worth are compromised in larger families. For example, many times the older children never have a childhood as they are co-opted into helping the parents raise the younger children. As we have said before, there is no substitute for a mother. Children are ineffective caregivers. The older child also resents being forced into caring for the younger children.

Some women just want the experience of having children but do not realize that it's not just their experience alone. For example, a lesbian couple may want children so one partner undergoes artificial insemination. I have treated many of the children who result from this, and they seem lost and unable to get adjusted in their life.

It goes back to good, old selfishness. Children need a mother and father to give them love, support, validation, and role models for direction. Granted there is a real human drive to have children, but much of it is societal and religious, too. Parents must decide whether they are mentally and emotionally equipped to have children. Couples must realize that, without care, sex can result in pregnancy, and be sure that they are ready for that.

A major problem is that people do not recognize that sexual desire is an animal instinct and, if not regulated, does result in pregnancy. And many unwanted children end up with dysfunctional lives due to being unwanted by parents who are stuck with the situation.

Many people run on autopilot to the point that they are "baby-making machines" but do not know what to do about it. It's all about taking responsibility, which is one of the major downfalls of your planet at all levels of life, not just in sexual activity. Often, lesbian mothers seem to be better mothers than heterosexual mothers because they really want the child, but it's too early to see the long-term effects and draw any conclusions. We have our opinions, but choose to withhold them at this time. Let time tell.

What's your stand on abortion? In my practice, I see many female clients who did not want to have a child, yet were driven by religious and/ or societal pressure to allow the pregnancy to proceed, which turned out to be a disaster for both mother and child.
In my work, I find that three out of five children are rejected before they are born, and that these unwanted children are responsible for much of the crime today. I realize that abortion should not be used for birth control but often it seems the only way out. An unwanted child no matter what the final outcome has been rejected and never bonds with the birth mother so it has three strikes against it before it gets into world.
Adoption does work some times but most of the time I find the child

cannot receive love from anyone as it feels it has no value. Children grow up feeling this way and have considerable trouble adjusting as adults because they have so many "I am not alright" programs that they continually self reject and draw people into their lives to validate how they feel about themselves. This happened to me even though I was with both of my birth parents. What about foster and adopted children?

This is a touchy subject when you look at how people react to the concept. The religions are almost unanimously against abortion on any terms, but the Christian view in particular has little validity. You are not required to have a child just because you become pregnant. All the fanfare and publicity by the anti-abortion groups affect people even if they reject the concept and support a woman's right to free choice. Your mind records and files everything unless you cancel it. As a result, it creates considerable guilt unless this, too, is understood.

Abortion should not be used as birth control. Reckless sex and the resulting pregnancy are not acceptable at all in any manner.

Often, an incoming soul decides not to enter the body, which results in stillbirth. There was probably nothing wrong with the body nor did the doctor err; the body simply cannot sustain life without a soul to drive it. Many times, the soul reevaluates the choice it made and decides that it was inappropriate so it departs.

If a prospective mother chooses to undergo an abortion, she should spend time talking with the incoming soul and explain why she is making the choice. This avoids guilt that can result if she is controlled or feels that abortion is not right, even though there may be no other way out of the dilemma. If she can forgive herself and learn from the lesson, it will be resolved.

You're right in your contention that people who were rejected before they were born commit much of the crime today. If children are not going to be accepted and cared for, they should not be brought into this world. On the other hand, many souls choose a disruptive family in order to create and deal with karma. Our major concern is whether the mother is able to deal with the birth effectively and give the child proper care. If not, then we support abortion as a method to avoid unwanted children. It has nothing at all to do with whether an adoptive family can be found; rejection by the birth parents does the damage, and even loving adoptive parents can seldom can rectify this.

Regarding the expression of sexual desires, sex is a base animal drive that gets out of hand with people who get involved with rape, child molestation and other forms of ritual abuse. What are the causes?

Those who become involved with these forms of abuse do not understand what's driving them nor do they even think about the potential dangers to them for acting out in this manner. The causes are anger and control, not sex at all, and can be rooted in a past life conflict between perpetrator and victim.

We have said many times that the victim must, *at some level*, agree to participate. Of course, this statement usually brings howls of outrage, for why would a young child allow itself to be abused? The phrase "at some level" is key, for you cannot look just at the small picture of the current time and the action. You must consider the soul's purpose and the lesson involved.

When we view something like this, we see the relationship between the players in the scenario, why they have come together, and what they hope to accomplish. Most people just see the perpetrator as a criminal and the other person as the innocent victim. But you cannot judge the truth until you can observe it from a higher plane.

How do you see sexual expression, desires, passion, and the need to express? How should we express our sexual needs without the result of children? It would seem that such a base animal drive must have some outlet, and if that outlet is via sex addiction, should not the person acknowledge it? Many people just want to avoid responsibility and say, "That's the way I was created."

Time for a history lesson. This again is a Western culture problem. In most native cultures, sex is strictly for procreation. The mother nurses the baby for up to four years, during which time, she usually cannot conceive.

Most people allow sexual desire to drive them rather than plan a family in advance. Most young people do not have the emotional stability to have children. Of course, there is nothing wrong with recreational sex as long as you are aware that that's what it is. It should not be the center point of your life. If it is obsessive or compulsive, then it is an addiction and should be treated as such. You must clear the childhood programs that cause you to use sex as a substitute for love. We keep expressing our opinion that sex is not love, but it seems to go over people's heads or fall on deaf ears.

From movies, magazines and TV, our society has become obsessed with love, passion, sex, and relationships. However, the media feed misconceptions and false messages to our children and young adults. How should we provide proper direction?

You cannot control all the influences on your children all the time, so you must build a solid, grounded understanding with them as they grow up. If you try to put pressure on them, they will rebel, yet if you try to avoid the subject, they will fall into the habits of their peers by example. If they have a loving supportive family that gives them proper direction, there is nothing to fear. But if they feel deficient in the area of love, they will look for it in the wrong places.

Crime seems to be increasing and getting more violent. It seems to be acting out anger and resentment. Do you have any comment?

This again is caused by breakdown of the family unit. There have always been criminal types who were driven by greed, and occasional out-of-control people, but as your society becomes more technologically advanced, its people become more separated from self. Much crime today is the result of an agitated, rootless society. You are now living with the first generation following the breakdown of your society, a generation that will have its own children, so things will continue to crumble right in front of you. But how many people will even acknowledge it? All you need do is look at your government officials. Need we say more?

Thirty years ago, the things happening now in political circles would have created a massive investigation and people would have gone to prison as they did in the Nixon demise. It's now, "Ho hum, business as usual. Do whatever you can get away with." What's your take?

We have very little to say other than your whole planet is obviously headed for some major lessons. We did not decree them or create them. You did. We ask you, "When you are going to wake up?" Your economy may look rosy but your society is crumbling. Your focus is on money, not on quality of life. What are you going to do about it?

The Roman Empire crumbled at its height. Did you get the lesson? Napoleon's empire crumbled when it was at its height of glory. In more recent times, the Soviet and Nazi empires have crumbled. A spokesman was sent to deliver the lesson plan 2,000 years ago. Many other teachers were sent to give you the message. Did you get it? We think not. When are you going to pull out of your downward spiral?

You might ask us, "What are you going to do about it?" However, we are just observers and commentators. It's really your game plan so you have to straighten it out. We are not your saviors nor will we intervene in your affairs, but will provide suggestions if asked. Your leaders seem to be driven by greed for power and control, something that in the past has resulted in the demise of many cultures and societies. "Is history going to repeat itself?" It's your call.

It seems as if some people are caught in a downward spiral and can't see their way out. Is there hope for these people?

Of course there is, but you cannot lead people out of the jungle if they even cannot see the jungle in the first place, or admit that they're lost in it. The truth shall set you free, but you must first be able to admit the falsehoods. It is possible to give people some direction, but they must want the help first. It's all a matter of choice and discipline.

This brings us back to the issue of believing something before you can see it. Is there a way that you can help people do this? Rather than change, many people would prefer to live in their illusions, denial and pain.

This is the major dilemma of all time and why your planet is in the state that it's in. People see the illusion as real so they feel that what they're doing is right. Common sense is clouded by the need for power and control so they see nothing wrong with their behavior.

Conversely, victims can't see any way out their fog so they let others continue to control them. As you have seen, change is threatening. Most people operate from autopilot so their mind gets locked into a pattern of following a program, something that requires no conscious thought.

Now, some people can see the way clear and are acting in right relation. This is all that's keeping your planet on track at the present time. But as long as people are operating from the delusion, they cannot see that their life is on the wrong track.

As we have said many times before, Earth is a free choice planet, and you are responsible for choosing your path. Once you find the right path, staying on it also takes discipline. The leaders of your country are not aware of their delusion, so they cannot possibly lead people to the right path. As a result, their people see unethical behavior as acceptable.

We can offer you no help or direction out of your dilemma. You are on a collision course with the destiny you have chosen, and the only way to avert the collision is by choosing to act out of integrity, ethics and honesty, to tell the truth, to take responsibility, and to reclaim your personal power. It is *your* responsibility.

Here's another illusion. Most people feel powerless so they attempt to gain power by accumulating money and control, to gain validation, authority and status by hanging college degree certificates on the wall, etc. Our society is so fouled up that it rewards sports figures with huge sums of money, which projects false values to our children. What do you have say about these illusions?

Very little. Again, it is your out-of-kilter society. It is so out of balance that it rewards the illusion that the physical plane is real, rather than rewarding true service to humanity. That is all we have to say.

How can we get to the point of self-empowerment so we can have inner strength, self-esteem, self-worth, and self-confidence?

You have answered that question in your books. You did all that it takes to accomplish that task.

However, it seems that my example did not make an impact. I have made some headway with my books, but a comment from your side might add some strength.

Are you saying that we did not provide the proper teaching materials?

No. I just felt that you could lend weight to my comments.

Could it be that people are not ready for what you have to say, or that they do not want to hear it?

That may be true, but I wanted you to validate and verify what I have said and written. For some reason, people seem to believe information from the other side more that they do from physical beings.

That is unfortunate, but true. We would like to see people become more open to the teachers that we sent, but people do not listen their own kind. Many times when the truth is taught, people do not listen, but they listen to fakirs and the pseudo-shamans. The mouthpieces for the dark forces seem to get their ear because they put on a show that is believable.

The next few years will decide whether our teachers are able to prevail.

There seems to be a battle going on between men and women for power and control. It seems that it's been going for millennia, as sessions with my male clients reveal traumatic past life events from a matriarchal era over 25,000 years ago that generated tremendous fear in their relationships. Is this true or an illusion?

What you depicted in *2011* is quite true. As you can see, the pendulum swings back and forth. Maybe this time, it will rest in center so there can be equality for the first time in your history.

Are we going to move past this gender battle to an androgynous state soon?

The time is approaching fast. Those who refuse to accept the new equality will find themselves in the Rapture as the Christians describe it, and will be taken to the spiritual plane where they can review their missed opportunities before trying again in a new incarnation. The cycle of return will continue. In terms of Christian belief, you are in a seven-year tribulation period.

Does this dichotomy exist in other galaxies or star systems?

No. As we said before, your planet is the least evolved in the universe. Other planets do not experience competition. Remember we said that the universe is evolving at a tremendous rate. Well, your planet is what's holding back the total transformation of the universe. Hopefully this will change as you approach critical mass.

This comes back to the statement that we are created in the image of GOD. Is that true?

This was true at one time, for all beings were created equal in the beginning and, at that time, you were the Presence of GOD. We are all the creators of this universe. Our image is imprinted in your file, but you got separated from your true Self, which you wrote over.

The program is still there but you cannot pull it up into the operating file. We are no different than you are; we just have a different viewpoint. Some of the people who were at your level have joined us, so if they were able to do it, so can you.

Were we given the opportunity to incarnate in flesh to see if we could resist the very temptation we have become trapped in?

Basically, yes.

Why were we not warned that we were choosing to take the path to oblivion?

You were warned on your first incarnation. In fact, you were warned repeatedly, but you were sure that you would make it through, even to the point of being self-righteousness. However, each time, you fell deeper into the morass of physicality.

You could see clearly before you got into the body, but you would lose or ignore your flight plan and come into life with little awareness. Admittedly, a few babies seem to be alert but, unfortunately, they are classified as problem children or slow learners, and educators dumb down their awareness so they become obedient. So many children are not in their bodies that the occasional ones who are alert and ready jump into life get singled out as "problems" and are treated as if they are abnormal. Your society knocks the awareness out of gifted children by classifying them as having "behavior problems."

You often refer to the flight plan we file before entering into life. I like the concept so I have been using it in my writing and work. Why do we lose the flight plan?

The last answer covers that quite well. Those who have the flight plan lose it because of how parents, teachers, and doctors threat them.

Let's take a different tack on the same question. Many of us are desperately trying to recover our flight plans, but getting them back piecemeal seems to take us years. Why doesn't someone from your level help us to recover our flight plan?

Your question shows that you are missing the whole reason why you are here in the first place. Have we not been saying that the reason you are here is to climb back to awareness of who you are? Are we supposed to just give you the answers?

You were the ones who tripped and fell into the hole. Are we supposed to pull you out? We have given you some tools to ask the proper questions so you can get back on the spiritual journey back to our reality. It is now up to you to use them. Life is a "do-it-yourself" school. Many of you call telephone psychics for answers, but very few of them are on the path. How do you expect another person (whose life is probably working less well than yours) to give you guidance? Granted some of them can tune in, but we reiterate that this is a self-help school. We have given you the tools, so use them.

Every once in a while, you get wound up in your discourse. I can see why because I have been promoting your concepts, yet few people will discipline themselves enough to use the tools.

We commend you on a good job of trying to get our word across. However, we are dismayed with the response that you and others like you have received. You have the answers but few people seem to listen to you. You have proven that your methods work without a glitch but few people believe in your work. The problem is that people are so locked into their fear that they cannot see the lesson before them. Getting back on the path and working through the lessons calls for the desire and the discipline to do it.

We see a chicken-and-egg situation, in that people dropped down in their awareness and experienced the very pain that is now keeping them at that level. It would seem that when you have something wrong, you must first acknowledge that you created this dysfunction. For example, people poison their bodies and environment and justify it as acceptable behavior. This causes sickness and disease, yet they blame it on something outside of themselves.

Of course, we cannot blame *all* people since the medical profession is the blind leading the blind into ever-deeper levels of non-responsibility. However, they do this because you hand over your responsibility to them. They obviously do not have the answers, yet people seem to hold onto the vision that they will find the cure. But after fifty years of research, have they found a cure for cancer?

Since we discussed birth and growing up, what about death and dying? I have my feelings about it, such as death is always a choice in that we decide how we want to exit this life. What are your views?

Your soul determines when it will leave the body, that shell which you inhabit for a specified length of time, so death is always a choice, just as life is a choice. Aging is a choice also. It is all a state of mind. You control all of it. Most people do not feel they have any control over life and death, but they are simply wrong. If you did not have the programming that caused aging, you would live much longer. The programming that causes illness and disease is the major block to doubling your life expectancy.

Stress is another factor that causes accelerated aging. The high levels of strife and conflict on your planet take a heavy toll on your health.

Where is heaven? Is there a hell or purgatory?

These are religious concepts that are used to control the masses. There is no place such as hell or purgatory outside of your beliefs; they exist only in your minds. For the comfort of the newly arrived soul, at death, an experience is created for you according to your beliefs. This is strictly temporary, and the truth is revealed to you during your orientation.

There is no judgment day, and you do not go before a tribunal where you are judged and possibly banished to hell as a sinner. Religious leaders created these concepts purely to control you, and they still scare you. For example, many people will live in pain, refusing to die because they fear damnation and hell.

If you want to describe the soul plane as heaven, you may do so for it has many heavenly qualities. But Peter will not meet you at the Pearly Gates. Neither will any of us be there to judge you. You will conduct your own life review to assess your progress. Unfortunately you cannot clear lessons on the other side but must return in a body to do the clearing. That is universal law.

Forgiveness is very big issue with many people. My feeling is that forgiveness is an inner-directed self-issue rather than forgiving others. My sense is that to forgive others is to let go of the attachment to the trauma or the resentment. Would you comment?

You are right. Forgiveness is not about other people at all. As you say, it is about releasing yourself from the resentment, guilt, anger, or pain caused by an incident. It is all self-directed.

What happens when people claim to forgive yet are still caught in judgment about an incident?

This another form of illusion. It is easy to recognize people who do not forgive. They continue to talk about the incident and cannot let it go. Their claim that they have forgiven is clearly false. The best way to check is Kinesiology, for the body never lies. A person may not be telling the truth but the Subconscious Mind will always reveal the inner feeling.

Does the GOD Source really forgive? Religions would like us to believe that.

As we said before, it is an inner-directed concept. The only person who can forgive you is you. It is not our job. We are not set up as a judge and jury over your lives and activities. That is your job. You create your own reality, whether that's heaven or hell on earth.

When traumatic events kept happening to me, I would ask, "If there is a God, why are you not helping me?" I felt abandoned and became angry. I thought the phrase, "Let go and let God," meant that when you detached from a situation, God would handle it for you. Many people still believe this. What's your interpretation?

This is patently false. We know that you would like to believe it, but the truth of the matter is that it's all in your hands. It has nothing to do with how we see it or respond to it. You can ask for guidance and we give you the best avenues to take, but you must decide for yourself what to do and then do the work. You must look at all the intervening factors that are working for or against you.

Again, remember that you create it all. These are the lessons before you that limit your life. Use yourself as an example. All the traumatic incidents ceased once you cleared the programs that were allowing them to happen. Do the situations still happen that were happening to you when you were angry with God?

You're right. I was in total control of all the things that were happening to me, but didn't know that at the time. Now I see how we can get caught up in the battle but don't realize that we're causing it all. Hindsight is 20/20, but when you're caught in a trauma, you can't see very well. Understanding that I was creating the circumstances was hard for me. Now that all the programs that caused those situations are cleared, I can see it very well.

When in the middle of a situation, it's hard for you to accept that you created it all, and to ask for guidance when you're caught up in the anger or fear. Most people do not know how to ask for guidance even when they're calm.

Fundamentalist Christians believe that all you need do is accept Jesus Christ as your savior and you are taken care of. Does that make sense?

This concept has about as much value as "Let go and let God." It is avoiding responsibility for your actions. Jesus Christ did not die for anyone's sins nor does accepting him as your savior do anything for you. It's the same old story of finding someone to lay the responsibility on so that you do not have to work for your own salvation. It is also another method that the churches use to control people, for they claim to be the middlemen between you and Christ.

Is there such a thing as the Will of God? Religionists are always talking about following the will of God. If you do not follow the will of God, you will not be saved.

The will of what or who? Well, again, it is a method of controlling people. You need an intermediary to speak for you, which the Church willingly provides, who proceeds to tell you what the will of God is. You must take the word of this minister, priest, or pastor as the representative of God. As we have said before, we do not have an exclusive right to the name "God." You are all GOD; we just have a clearer view of the universe. The only will of GOD that we know of is the Golden Rule: "Do into others as you would have them do unto you. Act in honesty, integrity and with ethical behavior."

How many people practice that in real life, including church leaders?

Many say that the white light concept is a trap set by the Satan and the Luciferian forces to deceive us, so that they can use it as a locator beacon to control us. Is there any truth in this?

None that we know of.

Are there Fallen Angels? Are Satan, Lucifer and the Devil real beings?

Luciferian forces do exist, as does Satan, but the devil is purely an invention of the religionists. Fallen Angels are what make up the Luciferian forces. These are souls who were with us but got attracted to the dark side.

Satan was created as the negative polarity of the universe. Everything must balance. The forces of darkness basically expanded that role. But you must recognize that your planet is the center point for all the dark forces. They exist nowhere else in the universe. All the dark forces have been attracted to your planet. Just take a good look at how the people in power on your planet operate. Do they act and respond as we answered in the question on the will of God? That is all we have to say for now.

On a radio show, a person who had written a book on Christian prophecy said, "There are people who are corrupted with the Anti-Christ DNA." What value do you put in that statement?

It is hard for us to understand people who make comments like this. In fact, these people have created the Anti-Christ by giving power to this concept. A person will definitely try to lead a movement against humanity, but he was created by humans allowing that type of person to amass power. As we said before, your society has devolved to a historical low in the consciousness from which you now operate. Just look at your business and government. It is not the Anti-Christ DNA at all but good, old-fashioned greed at work. Need we say more?

We will compile and write Book Two in the series and will answer questions that are of interest to readers who want to understand the human situation. Again, we are here to help but you must take responsibility and discipline yourself to use the tools we offer you.

If you, the reader, would like to submit questions to be answered, please send them to the publisher at the following address:

Personal Transformation Press
9936 Inwood Rd.
Folsom, CA 95630

We will consider all questions and inquiries. We are not able to return or answer any questions by phone or mail. Some may be posted to our website on the Internet. See Appendix D for contact information and website addresses.

Epilogue

In conclusion, where does having found GOD leave me today? My feelings now are very different from when I embarked on the journey to find the keys to the universe. I cannot say that I have found them all, but I feel close to the end of my journey. The last few steps have been arduous and, at times, I doubted my guidance but it has always proved accurate as long as I made sure I was clear and communicating with the Source.

In my journey, I found many "cosmic phone lines" out there, most connected to a dead-ends and some party lines with everyone talking at once. When I became aware that my phone line was not getting through the astral plane, I sought the help of Paul Solomon. I discovered that if I could tap into the Higher Self and the Highest Source of my Being, I'd get through to the fifth dimension and most of the voices would stop. There was little interference on the line once I'd found the right operator to help me tune in.

Developing the ability to contact the Collective Mind and the Akashic Record takes desire, intention, commitment, discipline, and consistency. Muscle testing opens up the Subconscious Mind, and once you learn how to use this process, the work begins to validate the information you're receiving clairvoyantly.

When you access the programs, patterns and records, you must have a process to release them, which is why I developed Neuro/Cellular Reprogramming, or N/CR. I worked on several processes at a time, and they all developed spontaneously together. The more I cleared my path, the faster my journey opened up doors to more knowledge. With the help of the first practitioners of N/CR, I was able to clear myself, and each time we cleared a block in my body/mind, a new avenue opened up in my work.

Tara Singh, a teacher I worked with over 20 years ago, said, "You will not teach anything you have not had direct experience with." That statement scared me at the time, but now I know what he meant, and can look back on the trauma and pain of my early years as resources in my work.

Yes, it's been a long journey, but you never have to traverse the same road again. However, the path gets narrower as you ascend, so falling into a detour without even knowing it is easier. But if you keep your eye on the goal and let nothing distract you, you will eventually make it. The journey is described in my books, *Becoming a Spiritual Being in a Physical Body* and *Journey into the Light*.

It has long been predicted that, as we enter the new millennium, every street corner will have its teachers, shamans, medicine people, self-styled gurus, and false prophets. It has also been predicted that many of these will fall off the path and fail in their mission unless they walk their own talk. Both are happening. As we've seen, we must live in integrity and be ethical and honest in our business dealings. People and organizations that ignore these tenets may prosper for a while, but then fall apart and disappear from sight. Sifting through the garbage to find the pearls of wisdom is an excellent lesson in discernment.

We must let go of any need to attach ourselves to someone else or an organization for power, validation, or approval. Many people get caught up in groups, cults, and programs, thinking that it will help them on their spiritual path. But often, the group and its leaders are bent on taking your power for their own validation. So, rather than your empowerment, the result is theirs at your expense. Cults are skilled at manipulation, and will tell you, "If you leave, you will be lost for only we understand you." In actuality, you are already lost if you need a group to make your life work.

Our challenge is to function within society, yet to be self-sufficient and reliant, making our own decisions, forming no attachments, and becoming a "no limit person." There's nothing wrong with belonging to a group, as long as you do not let the group psychology erode or override your sovereignty. If the leader fosters member empowerment, no problem, but if not, the group will be attracting people who are frightened by independence and need someone else to direct their life.

One of the hardest aspects of the spiritual path is being honest with yourself. We can go through life claiming that we are taking responsibility for the lessons that are placed before us, yet they come up again and again.

Denial and illusion are our toughest opponents, and our fellow travelers on the path could be our stoutest allies, but only if we can be honest with each other and make clear accurate observations. Then we could relay what we observe, without judgment, and we would all make faster progress on our path. The challenge is: can we do it, and will other people accept our feedback without going into denial, illusion, and justification, or feeling picked on or rejected? Both parties would need to exercise considerable discernment and commitment to pull it off.

Depression is caused by a lifetime's buildup of feelings such as, "I do not count. Nobody validates me. I am not all right. Nobody cares for me. I don't fit in. I feel alone, rejected and abandoned." Now, these could all be illusion or they may be real experiences that you never dealt with. They got pushed into denial-of-denial, and eventually build up to cause anger and fear that you cannot identify. However, as your life bogs down with these emotions, they will cause depression. Like a full septic tank, it must be pumped out.

You are writing into your records everyday. Do you know what you have written today? Is it supportive and positive, or destructive and negative? It's available to you if you know how to review each day's record.

Are you willing to devote the time to listening to your life and keeping a journal on how you're running it? When you decide to take command of your life, claim your personal power, take your power back, and assume responsibility, your life will change. The proof of the pudding is in the eating.

Miracles happen all the time once we know what causes them. *A Course In Miracles* is helpful, although I disagree with its contention that the Ego is the cause of most of our difficulties. My research reveals that the Ego has no agenda, nor does it influence our behavior. It is merely the file manger for the Conscious Mind's computer database. Most people, however, see it as the enemy, so it shuts down our short-term memory and our ability to program with affirmations.

One of my teachers once asked me, "If I could provide you with all the objects, qualities, desires, peace, happiness, harmony, joy, unconditional love and acceptance, and financial abundance that you're looking for in your spiritual journey, would you go with me? Of course, you would need to give up everything you own or are attached to, including your family, house, car, and social position?"

After a few days thought, I finally said, "Yes I would go with you."

We used Kinesiology to determine whether this was a deep commitment or just my Conscious Mind playing games. We found the commitment solid at every level, with no fear blocking it. The teacher then said, "Okay, you can have all those things, but you do not have give anything up since you are truly *willing* to give it up."

My Middle Self, autopilot, and Inner Selves were not ready for this abrupt change, and this reversal caused a major physical breakdown in my life. My book *Becoming a Spiritual Being in a Physical Body* documents the story of this incident; in fact, it was why I wrote the book.

Spirituality is about detachment and acceptance. When you master that, everything else falls into place: peace, happiness, harmony, joy, unconditional love, and abundance. All you need do is set your priorities, take responsibility, reclaim your personal power, discipline yourself to be consistent, and follow through to the goal. It is available to everybody, but most people cannot get out of the illusion to see it. Remember, you must first believe it before you can see it.

Happy landings. Just make sure you can fly before you take off.

Appendix A: Neuro/Cellular Reprogramming™
The Practice of Psychoneuroimmunology

> **Disclaimer**
>
> *N/CR changes people's lives. Although they recover from illness, disease, and behavioral dysfunction that are inexplicable in medical terms, we are not practicing any form of conventional medical practice nor do we diagnose or prescribe medicines of any kind. We do not claim that N/CR is a substitute for medical care. We are simply asking the body/mind to reveal to us the original cause, core issue, and catalyst that caused the dysfunctional program. When we find it, we delete and erase defective beliefs, programs and habit patterns. Then we rewrite the programs that control illness, diseases and behavioral dysfunction.*
>
> *You heal your body. You are the only person who can do that by your acceptance of the technique. If you are more comfortable with conventional medicine, then use that avenue. We do not advocate that this is the only way. Although we have seen many miracles in this work, we do not claim that any other process is ineffective.*

Psychoneuroimmunology is a process that encompasses all aspects of the body/mind/spirit in healing. Developed by Robert Adler in the early seventies, the technique explores the connection between our psychological aspect and the physical responses that appear in the body. Prior to that, little was known about the mind/body connection.

In 1978, I began my search for a process or a program that would clear my chronic back pain. I attended many workshops and seminars because the leaders said they could heal me, but nothing could permanently clear the pain. In desperation, I began to develop Neuro/Cellular Reprogramming (N/CR)™. At the time, I had no idea what I was doing and just experimented with hands on healing processes, energy releasing and other forms of healing. In 1980, I discovered that that all aspects of the body and mind were connected and that you could not treat them separately with any lasting results.

When I first discovered N/CR, defining the process was difficult. For 25 years, I had wandered through all the alternatives to allopathic medicine, looking for a cure for my own physical problems. I could not find a single person who understood my problem or could alleviate my pain.

I tried nutrition, but it was only part of the solution. When I discovered the power of the mind, I realized it was not what you put in your mouth, but what your mind accepts as truth. So I looked for a process that could get to the base cause of dysfunction without having to spend hours on a psychiatrist's couch as he or she tried to dig out the cause out of the client, who was unable to understand it in the first place. Most people don't know what their mind has stored, let alone understand it. Conventional psychiatry seemed bent on pinning blame on someone or something unknown, but I couldn't believe we had to be victims of other people's actions.

Initially, I had no idea that my physical pain was caused by emotional dysfunction within the programs in my mind. Like most people, I thought that physical problems had only physical origins; at least that's what doctors told me. Yet they did not understand why my spine was deteriorating and simply gave me the ultimate prognosis of being confined to a wheelchair.

At the time, I didn't know that my body was continually dialoging with me, and that if only I had listened, it would have revealed the causes. Physical dysfunction reveals *itself* but not its *cause*. Further, since emotional/mental pain is non-tangible, it is difficult to locate and work with. Also, I was not aware that my belief system had suppressed emotional programs that were causing my physical problem.

In my training with Paul Solomon, I approached psychology from a holistic, spiritual aspect; a very different slant from my original training. This opened me up to the dialogue and began helping me understand it, but it didn't heal my body. In a workshop, Ronald Beesley showed me how the body stores the memory and the basics of removing it. With this knowledge, I had the tools to integrate spiritual psychology with body/mind therapy.

This became the basis of my counseling practice, which evolved into Cellular Reprogramming™. In this approach, we released the imbedded cellular memory from past experiences.

Each cell retains its perfect blueprint so that it accurately regenerates and replicates itself. In the absence of any pattern of negative or dysfunctional emotional energy, the cell will regenerate perfectly from the blueprint. In 1988, I discovered that the Reprogramming process was actually erasing these negative patterns from past emotional experiences that kept muscles in trauma, so I added the "Neuro" prefix.

I discovered a holographic, body-based, spiritual psychotherapy process that uses affirmations, with love and forgiveness as the basic modality. We use Neuro-Kinesiology to locate the basic information we need to begin with.

This process works at all levels of the mind/body at the same time. We have four minds that network together. All the information we need is available from the mind/body. The body does not lie; it always tells the truth. It will indicate the original cause, core issue, and the catalyst causing the reaction, disease or illness. If you are living in denial or denial-of-denial, or on autopilot, we first deprogram the denial to get a clear answer. A sub-personality is usually driving the denial-of-denial, and can block any program from recognition if it is frozen in time in autopilot. We must go back to the time when the program was created and release the fear that caused the sub-personality to suppress the incident. Then, we locate the reason that caused the situation to be created.

In the future, N/CR will be a prominent healing process because it can address any dysfunction, emotional/mental problem, illness, and disease without pain, drugs, or surgery. No diagnosis is needed; all that's needed is the recognition and release of the underlying cause. Disease, illness, and emotional or physical breakdown are dysfunctional behavior patterns. Our delusion, denial, and irresponsibility block us from total healing.

In reality, there is no disease or illness. They are symptoms of a breakdown in our ability to understand what we are refusing to observe about ourselves. When we recognize the base cause and are willing to let go of it, healing can take place. There is no need to suffer or die to get away from taking responsibility for the lessons that are placed before us.

The basic concept in N/CR practice is to release the causes and core issues that block us from the truth about ourselves. When we see who we really are and recognize that we are all right as we are, no matter what the past discloses, we can reclaim our personal power and empower ourselves to take responsibility for our lives. Then we can begin to love and forgive ourselves. N/CR is not about paying lip service to make us look good, but about telling the truth about ourselves and accepting ourselves as we are without the need for control, authority or manipulation over anyone.

The miracle of the human mind is actually shared among a number of minds:

- The Subconscious Mind contains a detailed and faithful record of everything that has ever happened to you in your life, real or imagined. When we understand the awesome power of the Subconscious Mind to disable our immune system, we will begin to recognize how disease is created. If the Subconscious Mind holds false beliefs, concepts, attitudes or interpretations, they will create programs that drive our lives automatically, without any conscious thought on our part. Your body is the "hardware" of your Subconscious Mind, and the "software" is any program installed in the mind.
- The Instinctual Mind is just that: if you go into survival mode, it takes over. It has no ability to think, process, or make rational decisions.
- The Conscious Mind is the rational decision-maker but it, too, can also hold false beliefs and concepts you are not aware of. If you do not question these beliefs, they will run your life. Ideally, the conscious mind is on track all the time, but if you "space out" and go on autopilot, the Middle Self and the Subconscious Mind will take over, because somebody has to be at the wheel.

We are finding that, each year, increasing numbers of people are separating from their body, something we call, "a gray out." More seriously, "browning out" can cause memory lapse but you can still function. "Blacking out" happens when a person loses consciousness momentarily. This may be the cause of many single-vehicle wrecks—it's happened to me twice.

In our practice, we have also discovered that most people are running on autopilot more than 85% of the time. Our response to this is to seek ways to empower people to take 100% control over their life. With N/CR, we succeed most of the time, for we get the body to talk to itself so that we can reprogram the mind's various computers.

In all therapy processes, one question often seems to arise in the practitioner's mind: "Am I getting to the actual programs that stop us from attaining the inner peace, happiness, joy, harmony, acceptance, approval and love in the client's life?" Of course, the therapist must be in recovery himself, or the question wouldn't even enter his mind. In my interpretation, effective therapists must be willing to confront their limitations and issues which may block them from becoming compassionate, nonjudgmental, detached and supportive, with no need for controller authority over the outcome of therapy.

The need for control is the most widespread addiction we have today, and both therapists and clients react to it in an insidious way. If you're not in recovery, it's not an issue, but many people in recovery have an expectation or want to control a program, meeting, or another person's response, i.e., they are addicted to control.

As therapists, we are only able to guide and help our clients to understand the causes and core issues causing the dysfunction in their lives. In the N/CR process, therapists cannot sidestep their own issues, because they will surface along with the client's issues. In fact, therapists usually clear many of their own issues in N/CR sessions. You will recognize them and simply release them, because you are participating with the client in the release process.

We also need to have other practitioners to work with during our recovery. We cannot read our own book well if we are attached, blocking, or suppressing the causes. In my experience, even if we are committed to growth, we will block and refuse to recognize our attachments. Your body will always tell the truth, if you can get past the mind's blocks.

The final evaluation will only come in the results our clients manifest, as they traverse the path in their journey to transformation. With N/CR, we can go directly to the root cause and the core issues stored in the mind and locate these programs and patterns. We use Kinesiology and the acupuncture points in the body as gates, switches or entry points to release the information. In a short time, N/CR can release and heal any dysfunctional behavior pattern, illness, disease, or pain. We uncover and release the blocks to attaining self-worth, -esteem, -confidence, -validation, -approval and unconditional love.

Lack of love is the cause of illness. The major problem confronting most people today is that they cannot receive love or love themselves. If love does not exist in our reality, how can we recover self-esteem and self-worth, let alone heal ourselves? When we separate from our Source, we shut off the presence of God within. Those who need validation from the outside will interpret any concentrated form of attention as love. In the so-called Münchausen Syndrome, people hurt themselves in accidents or cause illness and disease to get love, and even more staggering, in the Münchausen-by-Proxy Syndrome, parents will harm their children in order to get attention. We will suffer abuse, both physical and emotional, to get the attention we mistake as love.

We have experienced amazing miracles with hundreds of people, such as spontaneous release of disease, emotional dysfunction and genetic defects. Oddly, however, other people either did not respond at all, or the dysfunction would return. This led to the realization that *I* was not doing the healing, that we were not "healers" or even "therapists." Our only job seemed to be teaching people how to love themselves and receive love. We can help clients to preprogram the situation and rewrite new scripts accepting the past and loving and forgiving themselves and others. We as facilitators cannot install the programs; the client must take responsibility and shift in consciousness. We can help by developing the software and using affirmations to install it; then permanent healing invariably follows.

As a therapist, I cannot change the holographic image that clients hold about themselves; I can only help them make the spiritual shift, thereby causing the healing. If that shift is not made, the healing process will give clients a temporary release. N/CR will work in spite of itself, because we are not working with the Conscious Mind. As a result, we are able to duplicate the process with different people in about 95 percent of cases, but there will always be that 5 percent who will refuse to take responsibility or reject the modality altogether.

When you take control of your life, your Subconscious Mind will cooperate with you, but many times, the Instinctual Mind will try to keep you in survival mode as it was originally programmed to. In an N/CR session, we must ask it to abide by our will by talking to it with an affirmation.

Middle Self is another matter altogether. If Middle Self interferes, we use a different approach to make friends with it so that it won't sabotage you. N/CR accesses the Middle Self's programming and gets it to recognize you as the computer programmer.

I have found that it is not the modality that causes healing to happen, since many allopathic and alternative therapies have claimed provable visible healing. However, they cannot explain why remission happens or how to reliably duplicate the process.

Psychiatrists, doctors, psychologists and practitioners have long recognized the need to release negative emotions. N/CR is a controlled process that gets to the core issue. Double blind treatments with different practitioners working with N/CR have shown that each practitioner has virtually the same experiences.

As practitioners, our effectiveness depends on our ability to get in touch with our clients' "feeling selves." We must build trust, so that our clients feel that we care about and love them. This trust is what allows healing to occur. One thing, and one thing only, governs healing: LOVE, and it works every time.

In Level One training, we focus on effective use of Behavioral Kinesiology and listening techniques for the body/mind. We communicate through Kinesiology and intuitive listening. Verbal communication is done through affirmations. When we locate the causes and core issues of the dysfunction, we communicate with specific affirmations, which are tailored to reprogram the Subconscious Mind. We have developed a body-map over the last ten years, which indicates the locations of most emotions (see Figures 1 and 2).

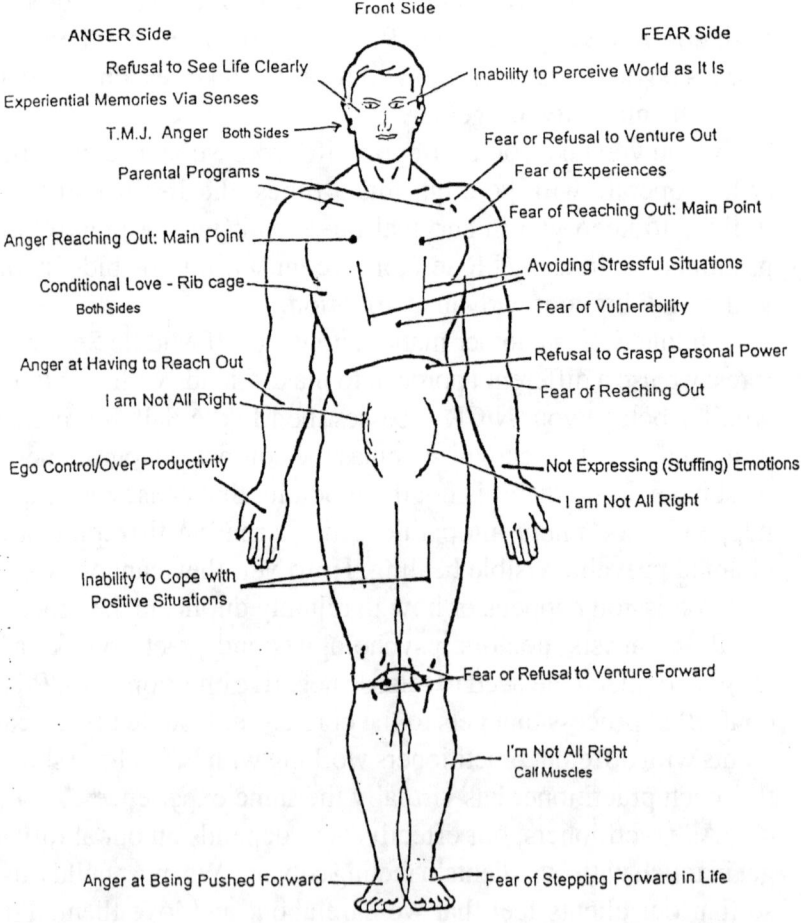

Figure 1: Front Side

As Figures 1 and 2 show, fear is stored on the left side of the body; anger on the right, with rejection along the spine. In fact, we have uncovered sixty individual locations for specific other emotional, dysfunctional programs.

As if the universe is trying to give us the answer, many doctors and medical researchers are discovering the answers to the puzzle of healing. In a *Discovery* magazine article called "A Bug in the System," scientists reported on the causes of disease syndrome. But they have no cure, prognosis or correction; they have

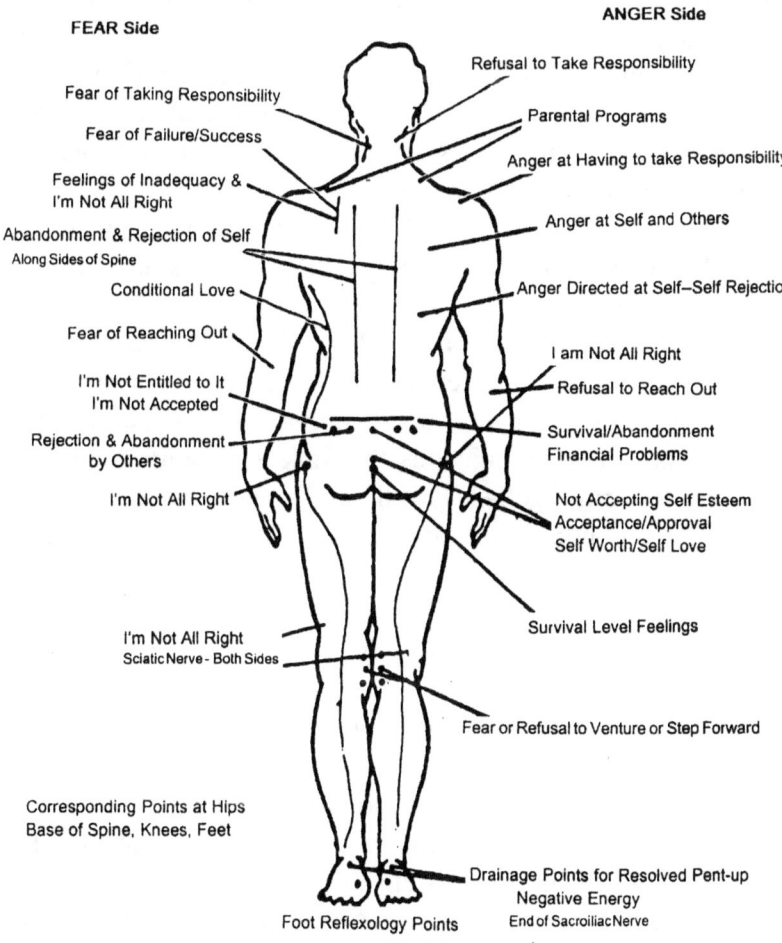

Figure 2: Back Side

labeled it "a genetic defect." Cellular breakdown is caused by the cell's mitochondria losing the ability to process and absorb nutrients. The doctors attribute this cellular breakdown and malfunction simply to genetic defects. However, regardless of why the cell loses its original blueprint, N/CR erases the cellular memory of rejection and lack of love, and helps the cell recover its original blueprint, so it replicates healthy new cells.

With counseling, physical therapy and almost all alternative therapies, we can remove the energy causing the pain or discomfort but, if we do not treat the root cause, we are just releasing a symptom. We have just masked the problem until the same catalyst or stimulus recurs and causes the energy to build up again, reactivating the disease or dysfunctional emotional program. With N/CR, we locate the core issue, uncovering the belief and/or the Subconscious Mind's program.

When the Subconscious Mind files an experience, it creates a record and program, with energy that makes small chemical changes in the body.

Many scientific studies in the field of Psychneuroimmunolgy have validated this. Two chemicals that activate neurotransmitters cause these changes—neuropeptides, the special chemical mediators and communicators that link the brain/mind and the immune system together. Our thoughts, feelings, and emotions affect our autonomic nervous system. Our mental states activate these specific thought, emotion, and feeling messenger neuropeptides. Because they are bi-directional in their action, they can function in reverse, affecting our behavior and mental state when we try to block or deny negative feelings and emotions.

Cytokinins are the second chemical in the equation. These are also bi-directional and negatively or positively influence both the immune system and the endocrine system. Working on the cell surface receptors, cytokinins either stimulate or inhibit the immune and endocrine systems. Negative attitudes, feelings, thoughts, and actions depress these systems to produce an inhibitory effect, causing illness, disease and/or depression. Over-stimulation of cytokinins from feeling depressed can cause endocrine and immune system burn out. This has the same effect that diabetes has on the pancreas. As a result, the NK cells will suppress the production of T-cells that interact with and destroy disease, virus, bacteria, cancer cells and pollutants.

On the opposite side, normal stimulation from happy, joyous and harmonious feelings and attitudes will promote health and wellness. The cytokinins will cause an increase in the production of NK cells and support balancing the immune and endocrine systems, strengthening them to ward of illness, disease and depression.

Each program remembers how we reacted or responded to the incident the first time it occurred. Each time we encounter this situation in the future, we access past patterns to guide our reaction, which reinforces the pattern that determines how we will handle future situations. Eventually these accumulated chemical changes will cause a physical breakdown somewhere in the body.

To release the dysfunctional emotion and program, we must understand the cause, and the reason why you originally reacted the way you did. When we understand the dialogue between your Subconscious Mind and your body, we can "unhook" that dialogue and release it. Then we erase the program's operating instructions, destroy the patterns, and file the record, pattern and program in the Subconscious Mind's archives. At this point, the energy is released and the behavior program is no longer accessible to you.

At the physical level, the cellular memory is released, which allows the muscle or organ to return to its original form. In the case of muscle pain, emotional trauma short-circuited a meridian, which caused the muscle to go into contraction. At the same time, the neuro-pathways were created from the experience. When the trauma is removed, all the effects are released and erased. The original program for the muscles takes over again, and the pain ceases.

In the case of a life-threatening, dysfunctional program, the same process happens. The original endocrine system programs are restored, so the immune system can rebuild the T-cells and leukocytes to destroy the dysfunctional invading cells.

All the physical programs are controlled by the Conscious Mind's computer, i.e., the Subconscious Mind. But because the body is a hologram, all levels must be addressed at the same time. We must work with physical, mental, emotional, and spiritual levels simultaneously, otherwise the treatment will be symptomatic and temporary.

N/CR will access the root cause, because it requires practitioners to get in contact with the client's "feeling self." By doing so, we can listen to information in the Subconscious Mind, which it deposited in muscles, organs, and acupuncture points. We use acupuncture points as switches to "turn on the video and audio," and allow the Subconscious Mind to bring the pictures and experience up to conscious awareness. This, however, is where the similarity with other therapy processes stops because with N/CR, we listen to body/mind and go directly to base cause. Then we get a clear understanding of the cause of the dysfunction. By describing the situation that caused the dysfunction, and then by getting the client to repeat an affirmation, the blockage is released.

My experience with Science of Mind helped me understand and harness the power of affirmation as the key to releasing and filing the record, program and pattern.

The focus of most therapy today, regardless of technique, is to release or suppress the symptoms; unfortunately that does not heal the body. Most practitioners expect some form of remission, cure or healing but, if they don't access the root cause, any improvement will be temporary and symptomatic.

Many people recognize the need to release emotional memories stored in their cells, but few achieve results. Cathartic release does not always indicate that the base cause or core issue has been revealed. Disease and dysfunctional emotional behavior patterns are directly caused by the lack of ability to accept oneself as all right and the refusal to give and receive love! Love can heal anything. To reverse the disease process, we must understand unconditional love and accept it.

Fear, anger, and rejection are the base causes yet, as victims, we try to blame some outside incident, person, or virus. The mind can create any disease it chooses but the only process that heals is love. N/CR provides clients with a safe space to learn how to love themselves and release the blockages in the body. Then the self can receive the basic needs of all people: love, acceptance, approval and all rightness that foster self-esteem and self-worth.

There is hope. Recovery is possible in every case. The only catch is that clients must desire to take control and discipline themselves to do what it takes. I am a walking example. My book *Your Body Is Talking, Are You Listening?* documents many case histories of people who literally shifted their belief and were healed in minutes. For some, it took days, while others gradually improved over time, depending their willingness to let go of attachment to the core issue that was causing dysfunction, be it *anger, fear or rejection*, which results in lack of love. When the client reconnects to Source, love can begin to heal the body/mind.

When we understand that our mental state controls our heath and wellness, we begin to become disease-resistant. We are no longer contagious nor do we contract illness and disease. Every aspect of our life and well-being is controlled by our feelings, attitudes, thoughts, and actions. Thus we have total control over how our brain/mind instructs our body to react or respond to any given stimulus. A positive response causes the neuropeptides and cytokinins to produce health-supporting activity in our cellular structure. The research done in the field of Psychneuroimmunolgy has proven without a doubt that our mental state is responsible for either a positive response or negative reaction.

For more information on the subject of Psychoneuroimmunolgy, see my forthcoming book *Psychoneuroimunology: The Mind/Body Medicine Connection Book 2* to be published in October 2000.

Appendix B: What Comprises An N/CR Session?

We will be working with N/CR, Behavioral Kinesiology, and biofeedback, if necessary. We demonstrate methods to understand the dialogue, misperceptions, and interpretations that the Subconscious Mind has stored in its memory. The acupuncture points on the body are switches or gates. Putting pressure on these entry points turns on the mind's "VCR" and opens the dialogue with the Subconscious Mind's files.

We must resolve certain basic issues before we can begin the process:

1. The client must be anchored in the body. Many people are out of their body and are unaware they are not functioning in their body, especially if they are confronting a traumatic issue. However, once they know how it feels, they can recognize when this has happened.
2. Electrical polarity must be correct in order for Kinesiology to work properly. If the polarity is reversed, "yes" will appear as "no" and "no" as "yes." We cannot obtain an accurate answer until polarity is balanced properly.
3. Therapists must allow themselves to be loved and love themselves. Separation from Source will cause a lack of love, along with self-rejection. We must accept our entitlement to love.
4. We must find out if the three lower minds are going to work with us. If not, then we must rewrite and reprogram the tapes. We must get Middle Self to recognize that we are not going to destroy it, and to convince it to be our friend.

At this point, we are now ready to ask questions with Kinesiology, or go directly into program releases. We can go directly to the root causes and the core issues stored in the Subconscious Mind's files. This will reveal the programs that have become habit patterns that are causing dysfunctional behavior, illness, diseases or pain in any form. We can release and heal any dysfunctional program in a very short time with use of Neuro/Cellular Therapy.

I recommend taping all sessions for the protection of both therapist and client. Also, the session can be reviewed and transcribed. There will be many parts of the session the client will not be able to recall because the mind may block it out. Many people have found that repeating the affirmations will lock in the new programming.

Q. Why is this particular process so effective?

Unlike other therapy processes, the client is required to participate in the session. The client is not *worked on*. In most treatments, such as Rolfing, Trager, massage, acupuncture, and other body-related processes, you do not participate. In psychology, you will be asked what your problem is, but few clients know what the base cause is, so how can we work with a belief, concept, or a program when we are not sure of the cause? The body will always reveal the base causes and the core issues if we listen to it.

We have to get Middle Self to cooperate with us, as it is one of the main players in the game. The Middle Self knows exactly what is happening in our life, so we need its support. All levels are brought in to play, physical, emotional, mental, spiritual and etheric, all at the same time. The body being a hologram, we access all levels of the mind and body with Kineseology and with clairvoyance to access the records that we need in releasing the programs. We go one further by accessing the ability of the Higher Self.

Q. What should you expect during a treatment?

To understand what a treatment is like, you must first understand what it is not like. No special preparations or clothing are required. You will not experience any deep tissue work that is painful, nor will you be required to accept altered states of consciousness. We do not use hypnosis or guided imagery. You will not expected to dredge up painful, emotional experiences from the past or "lead the discussion" as in analytical psychology. In fact, you do not need to tell us anything. Your body will reveal all we need to know, although we may ask some questions to establish some basic criteria.

Emotions may come up and you may experience flash-backs during the process but they are all momentary and release quickly.

We use affirmations as the means to reprogram and rewrite scripts in the mind. The therapist creates the affirmation, then the client repeats the affirmation. The only person that can reprogram your mind is you; there is no such person as a healer of others. You can only heal yourself. As such, we are only facilitators to direct the process.

Q. What goes on during a treatment?

When we locate the cause or core issue with kineseology, we must determine if it is a belief or reality. If it's only a belief, it may be controlled by a sub-personality. In either case, we can release it with an affirmation that will reprogram the software. If it is body-based, then we have to locate the acupuncture point that holds the incident we are releasing; a momentary pain will occur at that point. As we bring up details of the incident and forgive the cause, it will disappear immediately.

We do not experience the mind's action during the process; it instantly communicates to the body through neuropeptides and signals the muscles to let go of the tension. At the same time, it is rewriting the programs in the computer. Through affirmations, we communicate what we want to happen. It is important to understand that you are giving permission and removing the programs yourself. As the therapist leads you through the affirmation, you are healing your own body. The therapist is actually just a facilitator who has agreed to let you release the negative energy through him/her, providing an opportunity to experience love and forgiveness to release the incident.

Q. How long does this take and how much?

The number of treatments depends on your willingness to let go. Taking responsibility to see life differently without judgment, justification, rejection or fear/anger helps. A typical average is three to ten sessions. Some clients have had over 100 sessions, while others have cleared most of their issues in four to ten. There have been miracles in one session, but they are rare.

A session typically lasts about 80 minutes, charged at $75/hour. Call (800) 655-3846 for an appointment. If you are interested in spreading the word of this work, please call us. We would be happy to work with you.

Q. How can I become a sponsor?

We teach the Neuro/Cellular Reprogramming process as a series of five workshops. If you would like to help us present lectures or introductory workshops, please call the number above. We provide a free session if you set up a lecture for us (a minimum of ten people). If you are interested in setting up appointments for me at your home or other location, I will provide you with a free session for each day I work at your location. (There is a minimum number of sessions each day to qualify)

Appendix C: Attitude Evaluation

Psychological/Mental/Emotional Attitude Evaluation

Score on a scale from one to ten on each question. Insert what you feel your value would be on a 1 to 10 scale. Your answer in each column does not have to add up to ten on each line. Go over the questions again using a pendulum or with Kinesiology to get what your Subconscious Mind's belief and interpretation are. You will find a major variation in the readings. The ideal is to get a 10 on all positive traits and zero on negative traits.

SET POINT ANALYSIS FOR _____ DATE: _____

General mental Attitudes and Feelings

Negative	Positive
1. I am not deserving (_)	I am deserving (_)
2. I am not worthy (_)	I am worthy (_)
3. I am not all Right (_)	I am all right (_)
4. I am not accepted (_)	I am accepted (_)
5. I need to be in control to be safe (_)	I am safe and secure in myself (_)
6. I am not able to trust myself (_)	I trust myself (_)
7. I do not recognize my value (_)	I have high dynamic value (_)
9. I need recognition (_)	People recognize my value (_)
12. My self-esteem is low (_)	My self-esteem is high (_)
13. My self-worth is low (_)	My self-worth is high (_)
14. My self-confidence is low (_)	My self-confidence is high (_)
15. I am working hard (_)	I am working in balance (_)
16. Life happens to me (_)	I create my life (_)
17. Others are to blame for causing me to lose (_)	I draw all my lessons to me (_)
18. Life is full of conflicts and problems. (_)	I can handle the challenges before me (_)
19. I'm smaller than my problem (_)	I'm bigger than my challenges (_)
20. I have negative people around me (_)	I have positive people around me (_)
21. I am closed to receiving (_)	I am open to receiving (_)
22. I think small (_)	I think big (_)
23. I focus on obstacles (_)	I focus on opportunities (_)
24. Fear stops me (_)	I work through fear (_)
25. I have to fight for everything (_)	Life Supports Me (_)
26. I have to suffer to get to success (_)	Success comes without strain (_)
27. I'm comfortable where I am (_)	I seek to grow and expand (_)
28. I don't like to talk about my feelings (_)	I can talk freely about how I feel (_)
29. I prefer to follow established rules (_)	I prefer to follow my own direction (_)
30. I have a hard time making decisions (_)	I make accurate immediate decisions (_)
31. I have a hard time taking responsibility (_)	I am a "take control" person (_)
32. I am reserved and distant in communication (_)	I am totally open and free in discussion (_)

33. I am not able to trust my intuition (_)   I am able to trust my intuition (_)
34. I always stand in the background (_)   I am always in the front row (_)
35. I gravitate to the outside of the room (_)   I gravitate to the center of the action (_)
36. I would rather analyze the situation (_)   I will take action now, see if it works (_)
36. My decisions are influenced by emotions (_)   Emotions do not affect my decisions (_)
37. I empathize with others feelings and trauma (_)   Others problems do not affect me (_)
38. I feel others situations personally (_)   I am compassionate, but don't get involved (_)
39. I like conventional practices (_)   I like new ideas and approaches (_)
40. I do not like criticism or judgment directed at me (_)   I am open to objective criticism (_)
41. I see myself as a failure (_)   I see myself as a successful person (_)
42. I see myself as mediocre (_)   I see myself as having value (_)
43. Life is a struggle (_)   Life is ease and flow (_)
44. I play to not lose (_)   I play to win (_)
45. I am sensitive to others' opinions of me (_)   I value others honest opinions (_)
46. I am comfortable the way I am I do not need help (_)   I always consider others' support (_)
47. I can make it on my own (_)   I will accept help from others (_)
48. If I ask for help, people will think I am weak (_)   I always ask for help if I need it (_)
49. I know all I need to know about life (_)   I am willing to learn and grow (_) 50. It does not bother me to leave things incomplete (_)   I like to complete my tasks (_)
51. I put things off rather settle them (_)   I complete tasks, communications (_) 52. I have a hard time expressing my feelings (_)   I express myself without emotion (_)
53. I tell people what they want to hear (_)   I say what I want to say clearly (_)
55. I put off confronting issues (_)   I address issues directly and clearly (_)
56. I would rather do it myself than ask someone to do it and cause a conflict by forcing the issue (_)   If it is someone's responsibility, I ask them to take responsibility to do the task (_)
57. I usually have all the answers I need (_)   I am open to opinions and support (_)
58. I have resistance to authority (_)   I can be objective in a conflict (_)
59. I fear being placed in vulnerability (_)   I can be open and vulnerable (_)
60. I fear appearing inadequate (_)   I confront every issue clearly (_)
61. I feel isolated and alone in crowds (_)   I am happy with myself (_)
63. Fear overwhelms me, I cannot take control (_)   I am in control of my actions and feelings (_)
64. I recreate and live with my past (_)   I released the past, live in the present (_)
65. I feel insecure and unable to create a new reality (_)   I create new opportunities everyday (_)

Feelings and Attitudes about Money:

1. I do not deserve money (_)   I deserve money (_)
2. I want to be rich (_)   I am committed to being rich (_)
3. I unable to become rich (_)   I am qualified to be rich, I am attaining it now (_)
4. Money is the root of all evil (_)   Money isn't evil, but a vehicle of trade (_)
5. I don't feel good enough to be wealthy (_)   I feel good about becoming wealthy (_)
6. Money isn't important, I do without (_)   Becoming financially situated is important (_)
7. It is more enlightened to just exist (_)   Enlightened people can choose wealth (_)
8. Spiritual people not entitled to wealth (_)   Spiritual people are entitled to wealth (_)
9. You can't be spiritual and wealthy (_)   Most wealthy people are spiritual (_)
10. Getting rich is luck or fate (_)   Getting rich is easy if you follow the rules (_)
11. Getting rich isn't a skill to learn (_)   If you set the goal and the intention it's easy (_)
12. I do not want to spend the time it takes (_)   I am open to learning everything I can (_)
13. Never enough money for education (_)   I budget my educational funds so I can (_)
14. Success gurus charge too much (_)   I decide how much value I am receiving (_)
15. You must work hard for money (_)   I work smart, not hard (_)
16. I work only for money (_)   I work smart because it is satisfying (_)
17. I can't keep money when I get it (_)   I use my money effectively (_)
18. I don't want to struggle for money (_)   Money comes to me with ease (_)
19. Money creates pain and anguish (_)   Money creates Joy and Happiness (_)
20. If I really tried to make money, I would fail so why try (_)   I always succeed at every task (_)
21. People will try to take my money (_)   I don't associate w/ unethical people (_)
22. I must control my money (_)   I can invest my funds. If I lose, I start over (_)
23. I am set for low income < $30k (_)   I am set for moderate income $100k (_)
24. Am set for high income > $300k+ (_)   I am set for unlimited income (_)
25. I Am Set For Annual income of (_)   How much do you want? (_)
26. Saving money = scarcity (_)   Spending Money = Abundance (_)
27. Having money is responsibility (_)   Responsible people have money (_)
28. If I have wealth someone will have less (_)   My wealth has no effect on others (_)
29. I mismanage my money (_)   I am managing my money (_)
30. I pick losing investments (_)   I pick winning investments (_)
31. I have kow net worth (_)   I have moderate net worth (_)
32. I have high net worth (_)   I have unlimited net worth (_)
33. I am a business failure (_)   I am a business success (_)

34. I am an employee; I need a job ( ) I am an entrepreneur/owner ( )
35. I'm paid for my time ( ) I'm paid for my results ( )
36. My decisions are influenced by my emotions ( ) Emotions do not affect my decisions ( )
37. I empathize with others' feelings/traumas ( ) Others' problems do not affect me ( )
38. I feel others' situations personally ( ) I am compassionate and don't get involved ( )
39. I like conventional practices ( ) I like new ideas and approaches ( )
40. People should only have as much money as they need to live comfortably ( ) There is no limit the money you can have ( )
41. I have potential for wealth, I just need a break ( ) I create my opportunities for wealth ( )
42. Rich people did something bad or dishonest to get their wealth ( ) Wealthy people earn their money sharing and teaching others ( )
43. To be wealthy you have to use people and take and advantage of them. ( ) Wealthy people provide employment for and contribute to the welfare of others ( )
44. Money isn't really important ( ) Money is the vehicle that creates the economy ( )
45. I don't want to fight over money ( ) Balanced people don't fight over money ( )
46. When I get money people take it from me ( ) Wealthy people donate money to charity ( )
47. Money is freedom, I can't handle it so I will never have freedom ( ) Money provides freedom if I handle it right ( )
48. Money can buy health, happiness ( ) Health and happiness are developed qualities ( )
49. I don't have money, I never have Money doesn't buy health, happiness ( ) happiness ( )
50. If you are rich in love, healthy and happy you do not need a lot of money ( ) Love and Happiness are desirable qualities but they don't pay the bills. ( )
51. I do not want to be identified with wealthy, rich greedy people ( ) Many wealthy people are supportive caring people. ( )
52. To help people I have to be one of them ( ) Wealthy people would rather pay others ( )
53. Chances are that if you're not born into a rich family won't become rich ( ) It is not about birth, it is about desire, drive, intention, commitment and discipline ( )
54. Most of the good opportunities are gone. ( ) We make create our own opportunities ( )
55. You can't get rich doing with what you love ( ) People get rich doing what they choose ( )
56. As a women, it's hard to become rich ( ) More women are becoming rich all the time ( )
57. Given my background it is difficult to accumulate money and wealth ( ) We create our own opportunities by setting goals and using our discipline to achieve them. ( )

58. I am always giving, but have a hard time receiving. I do not want to be indebted ( ) — By giving and sharing I know I will receive a ten fold return. ( )
59. I do not have the time it takes to learn new ideas and concepts ( ) — I am always learning new concepts, and applying them to my success ( )
60. Money is hard to hold onto. I always have more days than money ( ) — My capacity to earn, learn, hold and grow financial resources expands every day. ( )
61. I wish I did not have to deal with money ( ) — I deal with money effectively ( )
62. I'm not smart or intelligent enough to get rich ( ) — All it takes is discipline and commitment ( )
63. Conventional values keep you safe ( ) — I create my own set of values ( )
64. I find it hard to take risks ( ) — The only way to succeed is to risk ( )
65. If I reach out too far, I'll fail ( ) — I know no limits; I trust myself ( )
66. I am suspicious of people who offer to help ( ) — I am open to support and help ( )
67. Success is an illusion in my life ( ) — I'm committed to set my intention ( )
68. Goals never work for me so I never write them for fear that I will fail to achieve them. ( ) — I set goals and follow through with Intention, commitment, drive and discipline ( )

When I Was a Child, I Was Told:

1. "Money does not grow on trees." ( )
2. "Save your money for a rainy day you may need it." ( )
3. "We never have enough money so don't ask." ( )
4. "You must work hard for money." ( )
5. "You must be very careful and guard your money or you will lose it." ( )
6. "Money is freedom, but if you never have enough or never have freedom." ( )
7. "You better get a good education or you will never have any money." ( )
8. "Money does not buy happiness be satisfied with what you have." ( )
9. " Rich people are lucky; they get all the breaks." ( )
10. "We do not want to be identified with those greedy rich people."
11. "Rich people will take advantage of you be careful if you work or do business with them." ( )

Money represents to me
1. Anger ( )
2. Fear ( )
3. Pain ( )
4. Loss ( )
5. Anxiety ( )

I attain from having money:
1. Purpose ( )
2. Contribution ( )
3. Happiness ( )
4. Joy ( )
5. Peace ( )

Goals and Intentions on Physical Fitness: Diet, and Nutrition for optimum Health

1. I am committing myself to 20 minutes of exercise each day. (_)
2. I am setting my goal and intention to build up to one hour of exercise each day. (_)
3. (If you smoke) I am committed to stopping smoking now. (_)
4. I am committed to stopping consuming alcohol now. (_) Occasional wine with meal accepted.
5. I am setting my intention to begin a new dietary program eating a nutritionally balanced diet. (_)
6. I am setting a goal to bring my weight into alignment with my perfect maintenance body weight. (_)
7. My body weight set point body is (_____).   My ideal set point for maintenance body weight is (_____).
8. I am willing to set up a dietary program that follows the best possible balanced program. (_)
9. I am committed to follow the Guidelines of Food Combining for perfect health (_)
10. My goal is to reverse the aging process to become younger. (_)
11. My chronological age is (_____) My physical body age is (_____)

Depending your physical health; diet/exercise, stress level and the toxic level of your body, your physical body age can be lower than your chronological age or older.

Recommendations for Proper Diet and Nutrition

Excess weight is epidemic today. Over 65% of the population is overweight, on the verge of obesity. Obesity in children has risen 300% in the last 20 years. Medical research and autopsies performed on young people under 25 years of age who have died from accidents, heart attacks, war casualties and other diseases reveal their physical bodies were equivalent to a person 50 to 60 years old. Cardiovascular blockages are as high as 50 to 80 %. This is the tragic effect of a junk food diet. It started about 45 years ago with advent of fast food restaurants.

To reduce weight, the body's thermogenesis must be working. This is the ability for the endocrine system to set up a process for the body to burn fat and oil. It controls metabolism and the body's heat factor which oxidizes and burns off excess carbohydrate build-up that causes excess weight. In overweight or obese people, it is shut down. The chemical response that allows the body to oxidize fat is turned off. The Chinese herb Mu Huang is the only ingredient that will reactivate the thermogenic process. Long, strenuous workouts over two hours and long-distance running will activate it through building up heat and activating the brain chemicals responsible for fat-burning . It makes no difference what diet or what exercise program you follow; you will not reduce your weight no matter how hard you try if your metabolism and thermogenesis are not functioning properly. We are working with a complex intricate computer that controls all the body's functions. It works well when it is operating correctly with programs in place. Our computer must have all programs operating correctly or the desired result will not be able to be reached. It is very easy to reset the weight maintenance set point with an affirmation.

Many researchers have claimed obese people are genetically set up or deficient in some areas which control metabolism. In reality, it is patterning that happens from family habits. If you set a pattern in your diet lacking in proper nutrients, it programs your body to set up your system to have slow metabolism and slow oxidizing of fat and carbohydrates. Overweight people tend to gravitate to foods that cause excess weight. All you have to do is observe people in a salad bar-style restaurant. Overweight people pick the high-carb food and eat very little of low-carb salads.

Another factor is lack of love. People from dysfunctional families who felt rejected, abandoned, abused or did not get love as children will gravitate toward sweets and high-carb food as it provides sugar which is a substitute for love. When they feel alone or rejected, they will go for food that satisfies the needy feeling. This builds a pattern that will begin to set up basic eating habits. If the parents have this pattern in place, they hand it down to their children. As a result their bodies then get patterned to desire the nutrient-lacking food. The body then begins to function and survive on sugar. It sets up a program to extract sugar from all the food we eat. When a person goes on a high-protein, low-carb, low-fat diet, it deprives the body of sugar so they are hungry all the time. When we reinstall the love program so they can love themselves and receive love, this craving goes away as the body no longer is needy for the love substitute. Since the thermogenesis is shut down and metabolism is slow, they have to be ungraded so they are functioning again.

To set up the weight reduction program, we have to check for the thermogenesis program and make sure it is not blocked by a program. Check metabolism and make sure it is not blocked by programs. Then we can delete and erase the current body weight-set point. We then reset the set-point for ideal body weight with an affirmation. If the lymph system is plugged up with toxins, we cannot get the garbage collector to remove toxins from the body. Most people are so toxic they need to do a six-week cleansing program. Once we get all the body's organs working properly, plus the programming set up properly, then weight loss will work well.

Suggestions to follow for perfect heath

1. Check your urine pH (acid/alkaline balance) with litmus paper every morning. If it is below 6.5, then you need to alkalyze your body. If it is down around 4.5, you are poisoning yourself with toxins.
2. Beef, lamb, pork and veal are very hard to digest. It takes digestive acid stronger than the acid in your car battery to digest. This can cause a build-up of toxins in the body due to incomplete digestion. Consuming empty carbs (white flour based food) and potatoes with heavy protein such as animal meat will cause the meat to putrefy and create toxins due to incomplete digestion.
3. Diets should contain up to 60% vegetables (preferably raw) no more than 20% protein and at least 20% fruit. Up to 20% of the vegetables can be interchanged with fruit.
4. Limit pre prepared foods from boxes and cans.
5. Eliminate frozen foods as much as possible.
6. Use fresh juices. Juices from concentrate, either frozen or bottled, are reduced to sugar and water when they are heated. The water is boiled off to make concentrate, so do not use.
7. It is preferable to eat vegetables as raw as possible. Heating above 100 degrees destroys all the enzyme value of the vegetables.
8. Oriental cooking is the most desirable form of cooking. Wok cooking uses flash heating and retains most food value. Make sure no MSG is used in preparation as it is very toxic.

9. Do not consume white flour products in any form, such as pasta, donuts, white bread, cakes, pastry, and tortillas. If you eat pasta or bread, etc., make sure it is 100% whole grain with no enriched white flour. They must have the ingredients on the label. If you are on a well balanced diet, you can stray off it once in while with no negative effects, but do not justify this, as it will build a habit.
10. Do not eat carbohydrates with heavy protein as it will cause the protein to putrefy and not digest properly. Fish and some poultry are exceptions as they do not take strong acid to digest.
11. It would be in your best interest to eliminate animal protein from your diet. It causes toxins and has too much saturated fat. It also takes acid stronger than your battery acid to digest.
12. Do not eat foods preserved with nitrites, such as salami, pepperoni and similar types of meat, as they will change to nitrosomenes in our body and become very toxic.
13. Avoid chemical based foods such as fat free whipped cream which is just hydrogenated oil. Avoid soft serve ice cream which is fat free and has no milk products in it. It is not ice cream at all, but just chemicals!
14. Eat food in proper food combinations. Do not mix protein with fruit or any grain, nuts, bread or vegetables. This is a cardinal rule that cannot be violated. Eat fruit alone by itself. Exceptions are papaya and pineapple. They have digestive enzymes in them.
15. With food combinations properly set in our diet, our

body can function at its highest level of effectiveness. If we mix incompatible foods, it breaks down because it cannot digest foods that are not compatible with each other. Many times we have heard people say, "I have been eating this way for 40 years and I do not see any problem with my health." That may be true on the surface, but if we check the toxic level of the body and give a person a heavy stress test, we will find different results.

16. We are basically a grain, seed and vegetable eating species. We have a 32-foot-long digestive tract, which is the same as that of a goat. We can adjust to light protein such as fish and poultry. However, meat-eating animals have a 9-foot digestive tract, so meat passes through quickly and does not putrefy. Their digestive acid is so strong they can digest bones. Conversely, they cannot digest most grains and get much out of them, yet most dog foods are based on corn meal because it is inexpensive.

17. To understand food combinations, read the following books, and to get a clear understanding about food combinations, go to our book series *The Four Quadrants of Perfect Health*.

Suggested Reading List:

Herbert Shelton: *Food Combining Made Easy*
Harvey Diamond: *Food Combinations and Your Health*
Herman Ihara: *Acid Alkaline*

Contact information:

Energy Medicine Institute
916-663-9178
9936 Inwood Rd
Folsom, CA 95630
Email mailforart@gmail.com
Web site: www.energymedicineInstitute.com

For more information about Heather Forbes' books and CDs, her training and workshops:

The Beyond Consequences Institute (BCI) was created to educate and provide resources for helping children with severe acting out behaviors. Most traditional techniques accepted amongst nationally recognized professionals are fear-based and child-blaming. These techniques do not teach unconditional love and hence they send children into the world with corrupted and distorted love programs. The *Beyond Consequences* Parenting Model, based in love and scientific research, provides a simple yet powerful model for parents, even with the most difficult of children. Resources developed by Heather T. Forbes, LCSW are available at:

<u>www.beyondconsequences.com</u>

Appendix D: Tapes and Books

The first two books are available in most bookstores in the U.S. and in some countries around the world. The other five are available in spiral bound pre-publication format from publisher, Personal Transformation Press.

2011: The New Millennium Begins
$15.97, ISBN: 1-891962-02-7
What can we expect the future to bring? How do we handle the coming changes and what do we look for? Prophesy for future earth changes and new planet Earth as it makes the quantum jump from the third to the fifth dimension.

Your Body Is Talking, Are You Listening?
$15.97, ISBN: 1-891962-01-9
How the mind works and how to create software for the mind and reprogram it. The cause of illness, disease and dysfunctional behavior defined. Healing miracles and how they are available to everyone. Understanding the body/mind connection in relation to the practice of psychoneuroimmunology with 66 case histories.

Being a Spiritual Being in a Physical Body
$15.97, ISBN: 1-891962-03-5
The "operations manual" for your life. Recreating your life for peace, happiness, harmony, and joy. Changing from being a physical being having transitory spiritual experiences to becoming a spiritual being in a physical body. Letting go of the duality of life.

Journey Into The Light
$15.97, ISBN: 1-891962-05-01
The process of ascension and the steps that govern the journey to a light being. Looking for the missing link in evolution. Stepping out of the cycle of reincarnation.

Recovering Your Lost Self
$15.97, ISBN: 1-891962-08-6
The author's journey from victim to cause in his life. How you can find your true self and have abundance in your life. Accepting unconditional love in your life through forgiveness and acceptance. Coming to the point where peace, happiness, harmony and joy are reality, not an illusion.

Pychoneuroimmunology: The Body/Mind Medicine Connection
ISBN 1-891962-07-8

What is psychoneuroimmunolgy and the mind/body medicine connection? An overview of the modalities and processes. Integrating the concepts. Research on the modalities. The mind as network computer. Affirmations, software for the mind. Neuro-Kinesiology. Using muscle testing for clearing beliefs and concepts, programs, patterns and records that are causing allergies, emotional behavior patterns, disease, illness and physical breakdown in the body. Neuro/Cellular Repatterning, a method to access the mind's programs, beliefs and interpretations and release them to heal any disease, illness or dysfunction in the mind/body. Miracle healings on demand with love and forgiveness. Supporting the body with nutritional and herbal products.

Tapes

Tapes are available on the guided imagery to train yourself to access the records and on the process for contacting your teacher and accessing the Hall of Records.

1. **The Seven Chakra Guided Imagery:**
   Train yourself to step out of the body to enter the Temple and the Hall of Records.

2. **Accessing your Akashic Records:**
   On the process and the various forms and methods of finding the answers to all your questions.

3. **Psycho/Physical Self Regulation:**
   Originally a tape for runner and walkers to regulate, flush the body of toxins and burn fat for energy. Can be used to train yourself to eat properly and reduce weight.

To order, go to web site www.transformyourmind.com

Energy Medicine Institute

9936 Inwood Road,

Folsom, CA 95630

916-663-9178

mailforart@gmail.com

Appendix E: Glossary

This book uses terminology that is not in common usage today. This glossary will help in understanding them.

A Course In Miracles: a set of three books that describes how we can change our view of forgiveness and love, and achieve peace and happiness through understanding who we are in relation to the Holy Spirit. The teacher's manual tells us that we are all students and teachers at all times in our life. The lesson manual shows us how to change our concept of who we are each day.

Addiction: compulsion or obsession about a situation or a substance that will cover up, meet a need or avoid a situation. The paradox: getting too much of what you do not need to satisfy an emotional imbalance in life.

Ascension: an evolutionary process of becoming a light being through releasing all the emotions and control sub-personalities that drive our life. Being able to reclaim our personal power and become a "no limit" person. The final result is getting off the cycle of return (reincarnation).

Back-up files: each day, the mind backs up all its files just as you would with a computer to save and protect your files.

Clairvoyant, Clairaudient: using our sixth senses to see and hear beyond normal restrictions of sight and hearing.

Collective Mind: a collection of information from all areas of the universe. Could be also described as the Akashia.

Conscious Rational Mind: the mind that we use to input information and data to the Subconscious Mind's files.

Cosmic phone line: a connection into the higher forces with no discernible source.

Dark Forces: beings from the astral plane, commonly described as demons, devil, satanic or Luciferian beings.

Denial: the first level of locking up programs so you do not have to deal with them. They can be located in any of the four minds.

Denial-of-denial: when an incident is too traumatic to deal with, we lock it up in denial-of-denial so that we cannot access it at all. However, it can affect our mental state even though we are unaware of it.

Divination: gaining answers using any form of an instrument, such as dowsing, pendulums, or oracles.

Ego or File Manager: the aspect of our mind that files the records in and retrieves information from the Subconscious Mind's data files. (I prefer the term *Middle Self*.)

Grace: that which is accorded to us to clear karma. When we acknowledge we have learned the lesson from a karmic experience, contract, or agreement, we can claim Grace and the Lords of Karma will delete the lesson from our Akashic Record.

GOD: (uppercase) the GOD Source or Presence of GOD.

God: (lowercase) the Christian or religious reference to God.

Holographic Mind: the soul level of mind that is in direct contact with Higher Self. It has access to all the records in the mind and Akashic. Will provide help when you request it. The all-knowing mind.

Karma: contracts that are created by dishonest, unethical or out-of-integrity behavior. If you kill someone even if in the line of duty, a karmic agreement is created. If you harm someone in anyway, you create a karmic contract.

Kinesiology: a form of divination that uses the various muscles of the body to answer questions. When accessing the mind through muscle testing for answers, the neuromotor responses are indicated through either strong or weak muscular response depending on how you assign Yes or No.

Lords of Karma: beings from the spiritual plane that reside with the GOD Source and help us file our flight for each life. They maintain the Akashic Record.

Love: a manifestation of actions and feelings that support growth, happiness, joy, peace of mind and acceptance.

Middle Self: the middle mind made up of the Conscious Mind, Instinctual Mind and Inner Middle Self. All the sub-personalities are installed in the Middle Self files. Quite often, it is misidentified as Ego because it exhibits the qualities that people generally ascribe to Ego.

Mystery School: an exoteric school that has existed for thousands of years. Many teachers who have been given the information by GOD Source have carried the tradition on. The teachers are chosen by the White Brotherhood and GOD Source. Many self-proclaimed teachers have set up mystery schools, calling for discernment as to who are the true teachers.

Psychoneuroimmunolgy: a new concept developed by Robert Adler, a faculty member of the Rochester Medical School, where he is now Director of the Department of Psychoneuroimmunology Research. The basic concept is that mental states control the distribution and production of chemicals that communicate with the various systems within the mind/body. They control the immune and endocrine functions, which in turn control heath and wellness.

Quickening: the increase in planetary vibration caused by the shift in energy on the planet.

Spiritual Practice: a discipline one follows in an effort to develop spirituality.

Spiritual Journey: the path to transformation that entails learning many lessons in letting go of limitations, emotions, and karma.

Spirituality: the result of learning the lessons on the path; the process of becoming a person who functions with honesty, ethics and integrity.

Universal Laws: the laws that govern the universe. The specific laws are set up to control interactions and apply to all planetary systems and star groups. (On this planet, we do not seem to acknowledge this simple form of law.)

About The Author

In today's world, the issue of credibility often comes up. How many degrees do you have? What colleges did you attend? Who did you study with? Who were your teachers? How do you know this works?

When I needed outside validation and acceptance, those were valid questions. Now I do not consider them valid, nor do I care if others reject me because I don't have the credibility they seek. What I learned in college has no relevance to what I do now in my practice. What I know is far more important than my background. Therefore, I am not interested in listing all my credentials.

Neuro/Cellular Repatterning is a process that was developed by myself and three people who worked with me during the research period: Dr. James Dorabiala, Mike Hammer and Bernard Eckes. And new information still pours in even today. This is basically a self-taught process, and everyone who worked with us over the last 20 years are our students and our teachers.

What *is* relevant is that we be open to new ideas. I will attend others' workshops and experience their treatments. Healing is an open-ended and ongoing process in which we need to be open to new ideas. The "sacred cow" syndrome is out-dated and does not work for me.

Someone once attacked me with, "You think you have the whole pie, don't you? You believe that nobody can match up to you."

My response was, " I don't think I have the whole pie, but based on the success of the last 20 years, maybe I have a few more pieces than some other practitioners."

Art was born into a family where his father wanted a child and his mother did not. As an only child, he did not have any sibling interaction, so his only contacts were at school. His dysfunctional family laid down many problems, which he has come a long way in clearing, thanks to discovery of the process he developed—Neuro/Cellular Repatterning—and the people who worked with him over the years.

In 1963, he quit college after five years feeling frustrated with the educational system. He dabbled in real estate, but found that it was not his calling. In 1965, he married Susie, his partner ever since. Their sons, Ross and Ryan, were born in 1971 and 1976.

Very few people in the field of therapy work seem to be able to stay in relationship due to the fact they do not want to deal with their own issues. Art was committed to find himself and went on a path to do so. He stabilized his own relationship by working out his issues.

In 1968, he and Susie found themselves in St. Helena, CA, rebuilding an abandoned winery. To clear the land to plant grapes, Art became a logger. To support his family while the winery was being rehabilitated, he hired out his D8 Caterpillar tractor for land-clearing and vineyard preparation. After seven years, the big money interests were pushing grape prices above what was economically viable for a small winery to stay in business, so he sold the winery.

His next venture was a restaurant which he built himself, but found that the restaurant field is one of the most demanding there are. Despite instant financial success, he sold the restaurant after four years and moved on. However, Art met his first teacher at the restaurant, someone who planted a seed of doubt about his life path. At the time, Art was trying to find himself and was studying extensively and attending self-improvement seminars. After closing time, they would spend many hours talking about their paths.

In 1978, the buyers of the restaurant went bankrupt, so their payments stopped. Art had to return to work and his quest was disrupted. Fortunately, Susie was working full-time, but in 1980, she was laid off and Art, who had a green thumb, worked as a gardener at a senior citizens' complex. Having closely studied the Findhorn community, he took the opportunity to apply what he had learned about the earth spirits. He found, from the plants themselves, that the landscape architect had put many of them in the wrong place. Over the next year, he transformed the barren grounds into magnificent flower gardens, and even built a passive solar greenhouse to grow flowers year around.

By 1982, his healing practice was established so he quit the gardener job and concentrated on researching healing practices.

Art soon found that Santa Rosa, CA did not support the type of work he was doing, and when Joshua Stone invited him to go to Los Angeles to give readings to clients, he jumped at the opportunity. He and Joshua found they worked well together as a team, and Art was able to provide a unique and valuable service to many therapists. However, the traveling almost broke up his family, so they moved to Sacramento, CA, and opened a bookstore and metaphysical center.

While Art received considerable support for this venture, he didn't anticipate that few people had the money to support it financially. Having invested all the family's savings, and refinanced their house, all went well for almost three years until he took on partners in order to expand. However, his partners did not understand the law of cause and effect, and when they embezzled $30,000, the business went under.

Knowing that "What goes around comes around," Art managed to accept what had happened, forgive them and get on with his life. However, trying to understand the lesson in this was hard to accomplish. When you are angry at losing your life savings and 20 years of hard work, the clarity and acceptance that he had set it all up came slowly. Even though he knew this at one level, it was a hard lesson to learn. The lesson was that while he received much verbal validation from those who supported the center, he was paying over half its operational costs.

The failure was a mixed blessing. It put him on a new path, one in which he traveled and spread the word of his work, and really had to get down to business. He did finally recover, even though they lost their house and one of their cars.

Looking back, Art recognizes the many great strides forward that he has made. Today, he travels extensively giving lectures, seminars and workshops on a variety of subjects. He also has a circuit of cities that he visits regularly for individual sessions.

His publishing company promotes his books (see list in the front of this book), and they are available through the Wellness Institute.

www.ingramcontent.com/pod-product-compliance
Lightning Source LLC
LaVergne TN
LVHW051828080426
835512LV00018B/2777